MOTHER NATURE

ANIMAL
PARENTS
AND
THEIR YOUNG

MOTHER NATURE

CANDACE SAVAGE

GREYSTONE BOOKS

DOUGLAS & MCINTYRE

VANCOUVER/TORONTO

For
EILEEN

97 98 99 00 01   5 4 3 2 1

Greystone Books
A division of Douglas & McIntyre Ltd.
1615 Venables Street
Vancouver, British Columbia
V5L 2H1

Originated by Greystone Books and published simultaneously in the United States of America by Sierra Club Books, San Francisco

Canadian Cataloguing in Publication Data

Savage, Candace, 1949–
    Mother nature

    Includes bibliographical references and index.
    ISBN 1-55054-546-9

    1. Parental behavior in animals. 2. Mammals—Infancy. I.
Title.
QL762.S38 1997   599.056   C96-910800-1

Jacket and book design by DesignGeist
Front cover photograph: Norbert Rosing
Back cover photograph: Denver A. Bryan
Printed and bound in Singapore by C. S. Graphics Pte. Ltd.

Photo on endpapers: Cheetah mother and cub NORBERT ROSING
Photo on pages ii–iii: Porcupine adult and young TOM AND PAT LEESON
Photo on page iv: Alaska brown bear sow and cub DANIEL J. COX/NATURAL EXPOSURES

The author gratefully acknowledges the expert assistance of Dr. Peter Flood of the Western College of Veterinary Medicine at the University of Saskatchewan in Saskatoon.

The publisher gratefully acknowledges the assistance of the Canada Council and of the British Columbia Ministry of Tourism, Small Business and Culture.

CONTENTS

PREFACE

This book began with a straightforward proposition. "What I really want," my publisher said, "is an album of baby animals. People would like it; it would sell." "It would sell" surely meant that I would earn some money.

Although I make my living by writing books, I am not always influenced by such crass reckoning. Life is too short to spend it grubbing for cash. But even writers must eat; and writers' teenage children, it was becoming clear, must have music, movies, gasoline and the occasional four-topping pizza. More worryingly, my seventeen-year-old daughter was beginning to scour the secondhand stores for clothes to wear to her high-school grad, a sure sign that other, much larger bills were looming—rents, air fares, tuitions. My duty as a parent was clear. I needed a bank account.

In retrospect, this prosaic motivation has come to seem entirely appropriate for the project that has grown to become *Mother Nature*. Although I began work, as requested, with my eye on the very young, my focus quickly broadened to include their parents. We humans, I was reminded, are not alone in our devotion to the younger generation. In fact, every species of mammal in the world—some 3,900 in all—finds itself in much the same situation. While nonhuman mammals don't have to cater to the latest in tot-and-teen tastes, they are all obliged to provide food, protection and shelter for their infants and, often, for older progeny. Almost by definition, mammals are animals that take care of their offspring.

As a mammalian parent myself, I was immediately drawn to this subject and to the literature on mammalian parenting. Happily, it is a hot topic these days, and scientific interest is fueled each year by hundreds of publications, each designed to describe some new behavioral subtlety and to speculate on its evolutionary meaning. Why, and under what conditions, do some rodents selectively abort female fetuses? Why are male mice sometimes model fathers and sometimes total deadbeats? Why do prairie dogs kill their neighbors' pups when they're in the den and then nurse the survivors when they emerge above ground? Even though I've spent much of the last twenty years browsing through biological journals, I was constantly taken aback by new and unexpected aspects of animal life. Mammalian parenting turned out to be surprisingly quirky.

What I learned was not only intriguing; it could also be unsettling. On the whole, I enjoyed the new understandings to which my research led. For example, I was delighted to discover that animal mothers are not passive victims of their biological role, ever willing to sacrifice their well-being to that of their youngsters. Instead they are often ambitious, occasionally aggressive and, when need be, downright self-serving. This tough, practical image of mothering appealed to me. But I was discomfited by what I learned about the sexual division of labor among mammalian parents. For most nonprimate species, mothers do all the childcare—fathers none at all. The venerable "argument from biology" that, historically, has been used against human females was weightier than I had thought. ("Females are made for child rearing; males to master the world.") Yet this argument did not take into account the parenting practices of humans or their primate relatives, among whom two-parent care is more or less the norm. Was the argument freshly compelling or completely irrelevant?

As I read and thought, my questions multiplied. Why is fatherhood so rare among mammals? Why are infant abuse and infanticide relatively common? Has the transmission of knowledge from mother to young led to the development of animal cultures? How, exactly, do humans fit into the picture? What had started as a simple, hearts-and-flowers celebration of the beauty of young animals soon grew into an engrossing study that left my mind buzzing with information, ideas and perplexities. Preparing this book has enriched my contemplation of both animal and human lives, and I very much hope that perusing it will do the same for yours.

ALL THAT I AM,
MY MOTHER MADE ME.

NAPOLEON BONAPARTE, "SAYINGS OF NAPOLEON," C.1800

I FAMILY VALUES

IF HUMANS WERE MORE LIKE WOOD FROGS, our lives would be simpler. This is because wood frogs are naturally attuned to the concept of gender equality. When it's time to reproduce, males and females make a roughly equivalent contribution to the success of their progeny. Mother Frog leads the way by laying her eggs en masse, and Father Frog follows suit by dousing them with his sperm. Then, their parental duties accomplished for another year, the adults hop back up onto their lily pads and leave fate to take care of the rest.

Like many other cold-blooded animals, wood frogs have perfected the art of reckless reproduction. Their game plan calls for producing swarms of young and letting them fend

Although mammalian parenting can be a round-the-clock job, it is not without its obvious comforts. NORBERT ROSING

OVERLEAF Every baby mammal calls out for its parent's care, though few can plead their case as well as this little fox. ALAN AND SANDY CAREY

for themselves, in the expectation that a few stalwart souls will survive to carry the parental genes into the next generation. It's extravagant, but it generally works. In the face of calamities (plague, drought or flood), Mother and Father Frog look out for themselves and leave their offspring to get by as best they can. If the little tads all succumb, it doesn't matter much: there's always next year and another breeding season. But if bad times were to persist for many years in a row, something would have to be done. Nature would be called upon to create a frog that knew how to take care of its young.

Over the course of evolution, this is exactly what has happened. Here and there around the world, there are species of frogs that lay their eggs on land (a hostile environment if ever there was one) and then *carry* their tadpoles to water. There are others that stand guard over their embryos and hatchlings, and even a few that provision their young by laying eggs for them to eat. And frogs aren't the only animals that have been called on by adversity to cater to their offspring. Female pythons defend their eggs and, sometimes, their tiny newborns; cichlid fish of either sex may guard their fry by holding them in their mouths; and male seahorses "gestate" fertilized eggs in a special brood pouch. Although the majority of cold-blooded animals do not tend their young, limited parental care (by females, males or both) has evolved in a variety of insects, amphibians, fish and reptiles, from honeybees to crocodilians.

Warm-blooded creatures, by contrast, are universally and irrevocably committed to parenthood. Birds' eggs must be constantly warmed if the embryos are to survive. Greedy young nestlings must be stuffed with food to fuel their rapid growth. For most species of birds, it takes the flat-out effort of both parents to meet the needs of a nestful of chicks. Without this dawn-to-dusk investment, reproduction is quite simply impossible. And for mammals, the challenge is even more compelling. Although they produce relatively few offspring (compared to birds, say, or frogs), those few precious infants require intensive care for weeks, months or even—as humans know only too well—decades.

Thankfully, among people, the work of childcare is often shared by both parents, at least in some measure. But for most nonhuman mammals, the demands of parenthood fall almost exclusively on the females. Males assist with infant care in only 5 per cent of

Even the most competent of young mammals is dependent on its mother for basic life support. (Sadly for this white-tailed fawn, protection from mosquitoes is not part of the deal.) ART WOLFE

mammalian species, with the welcome exceptions to be found predominantly among rodents, primates and carnivores. Active fatherhood is therefore less common in mammals than it is in birds (where two-parent families are by far the norm) or even in bony fishes (among which fathers are more likely than mothers to tend the young). The typical mammalian male is little more than a highly evolved sperm dispenser, constantly on the lookout for a chance to score. Emancipated from parental duties, he is also excluded from parental influence and depends almost entirely on females to determine his reproductive fortunes. If Mother Muskrat fails in her care of Junior, the infant and its father's hopes will die in the same instant.

As evolutionary biologist Sarah Blaffer Hrdy puts it, female mammals "are and always have been the chief custodians of the breeding potential of the species." This extraordinary division of responsibility has been given physical expression in the flesh-and-blood of mammalian anatomy. As every schoolchild knows, the distinguishing features of the class Mammalia are milk and mammary glands, characteristics that are exclusive to the female body. For better or worse, ours is the evolutionary lineage that invented Motherhood.

The typical mammalian male is little more than a highly evolved sperm dispenser, constantly on the lookout for a chance to score.

Back in the Age of the Dinosaurs, when our ancestors first appeared (as scuttling mouselike creatures that hid in the leaf litter), the ability to produce milk must have been the answer to every mother's prayer. The jungles and swamps of the day were filled with dangers. Reptiles of all sizes and shapes kept sharp-eyed, sharp-toothed watch for mammals that ventured out of the shadows. How much safer to keep the young ones at home in their nest burrows, where they could be nourished with secretions from their mother's skin glands. In all likelihood, this spectacularly useful innovation was first achieved by some odd little furry creature that laid eggs and lacked nipples. The infants simply sucked the milk off their mother's fur. Although "primitive" in view of what was to come, these traits have persisted for hundreds of millions of years and are still with us in weird and wonderful mammals like the platypuses and spiny anteaters.

Snug in its mother's pouch, this baby kangaroo may receive free room and board (with milk on tap) for up to eight months. ART WOLFE

Lactation may help explain why the mammalian line has survived instead of following the dinosaurs to their unlamented demise. Since nursling mammals no longer had to forage for themselves, food-getting was left to the adults, who were expert and efficient. Little T. Rex Jr., however, had to fend for himself and may not have had the skills to cope with the suite of environmental disasters that ended the dinosaurian era. Or perhaps our ancestors had an edge thanks to other, slightly more recent advances in mothering. Sometime during the dinosaurs' reign, certain female mammals acquired the ability to "incubate" their eggs inside their bodies. Instead of plopping the eggs into nests, mothers held them within a uniquely mammalian organ, the uterus. To this day, marsupials (the descendants of this pioneering line) still begin life inside eggshells, snug and warm inside their mothers' wombs.

If the advantages of internal incubation are obvious, the difficulties are also considerable. Chief among them is the problem of tissue rejection. Because an embryo is not genetically identical to its mother (half its DNA comes from its father), the mother's body identifies the fetus as foreign and takes action against it. As long as a marsupial embryo is able to hide inside its shell, it is spared this hostile reaction. But when, at perhaps a month of age, it hatches into the womb, the mother's defenses are aroused and the fetus has to make an urgent departure. A pathetic little pink fingerling, all head and front legs, the newborn must then struggle blindly through a chaotic jungle of fur to the distant lip of its mother's pouch. Once inside, guided by touch and smell, it manages to locate a nipple and latch onto it. There it will stay for many months, until it is finally ready for its second, less traumatic birth.

Although we sometimes think of pouched mammals as an evolutionary dead-end, marsupial mothering is practiced today by no fewer than 266 species in Australia, New Zealand and both Americas. Their parenting behavior is in no way unsophisticated. A kangaroo, for example, often carries two young in her pouch at a time—a helpless newborn and a bright-eyed joey that is almost ready to hop out. The nutritional needs of these two infants are entirely dissimilar, yet the mother can satisfy both by providing different grades of milk from different nipples. Because they gestate their young so briefly and nurse them for so long, marsupials have become virtuosi of lactation.

Two or three weeks after birth, these opossums still look like embryos. The nipple to which each is attached will stretch as the infant grows, allowing it to wriggle and turn inside its mother's pouch. WAYNE LYNCH

But this heavy reliance on nursing has its disadvantages. Milk production—eating for two or three—takes an enormous amount of energy, far more than would be expended during an equivalent period of gestation. The longer the fetus can stay in the womb, the less its development will cost the mother. The move toward energy-efficient motherhood was finally made about a hundred million years ago (just yesterday in the evolutionary scheme of things) with the development of the mammalian placenta. Based on a creative reworking of the membranes inside a reptilian egg, the placenta creates a bridge over which nutrients and wastes can be exchanged between mother and fetus. At the same time, it serves as a barrier that prevents the mother from identifying the embryo as foreign tissue. The eggshell is no longer necessary and can be eliminated. As a result, the richly provisioned fetus can remain in the womb for many weeks or months, constrained only by the capacity of its mother's body and the width of the exit through which it will eventually leave.

If biology is destiny, then our destiny is to explore new possibilities through the use of our intelligence.

As evolutionary upgrades go, the placenta turned out to be a real winner. From the beginning, the chief beneficiary of enriched fetal nutrition was the brain—especially the cerebral cortex—which grew larger and more convoluted than ever before. As mammals got smarter, they used their increased brainpower to interact with each other in social groupings. (Among mammals, there is a demonstrable correlation between complex brains and a complex social life.) Group living, in turn, may have translated into group inbreeding, which led to the creation of genetic subpopulations and, in time, new species. Placental mammals have proven to be an exceptionally diverse and successful group, with some 3,600 living species that include bats and cats, hares and bears, porcupines and people.

Motherhood, which first appeared as a response to the challenges of the reptilian era, has served mammals well. Indeed, as placental mammals have evolved, their commitment to parental care has grown ever deeper. Primates—generally considered the smartest and most "advanced" of mammals—tend to bear very few young, to carry them through long pregnancies and to tend them during prolonged childhoods. What's more, care is provided not by mothers alone but often by fathers as well. This trend toward intensive, all-consuming, two-parent child rearing reaches its extreme in human beings. In this sense, we are the most mammalian of mammals.

Humans of both sexes are passionately inclined to care for young ones, and our impulsive affection extends not only to our own children but even to the young of other species. We lavish care on kittens and puppies; we ooh and ah over lambs, kits, fawns and cubs. We are touched to witness the tender and devoted behavior of animal parents. Indeed, our empathy and interest can become a little too fervent. Even supposedly dispassionate, scientific observers have been known to translate animal studies directly to humans: as if the fact that ewes "imprint" on their lambs and stags ignore their calves has something profound to tell us about our own behavior. These connections, though tempting, are rarely meaningful.

The whole purpose of human parental care—from the richly funded pregnancy, to the midnight feedings, to the lessons of childhood—is to grow and nurture a brain. If biology is destiny, then our destiny is to explore new possibilities through the use of our intelligence. This gift, in large part, frees us from the rigidity of our genetic inheritance and provides us with options and opportunities that are not open to most other creatures. As Shakespeare has it, humans as a species are "naturally unnatural." Although we are kin to other animals, we are also different from them and cannot expect to find ourselves exactly mirrored in their behavior.

Happily, the intelligence that sets us apart from nonhuman animals also draws us to them in curiosity and pleasure. What can we learn by studying the parenting strategies of other mammals? To answer this question, we will have to start all over again, at the very beginning of the sperm-and-egg game.

OVERLEAF There is something about baby animals that tugs at the heartstrings of people. These pretty youngsters are coyote pups.
GLEN AND REBECCA GRAMBO

II | AB OVO

FOR HUMANS, COURTSHIP IS A MUTUAL ENTERPRISE. Boy meets girl/girl meets boy. They size each other up, and nothing much more will happen unless both have stars in their eyes. But for some mammals, sexual choice is almost entirely one-sided. The males strut their stuff, and the females decide. Take wolves, for example. A high-ranking female wolf can be expected to breed with the top-ranking male. But if she decides that she doesn't like him, she may choose to accept a promising young wolf from lower down the social scale. A female elephant who is ready to breed will consistently rebuff the attentions of young males in order to save herself for a mature bull with oozing facial glands and an obnoxious scent, characteristics that identify him as worthy of her sexual interest.

The cares of adulthood seem far from the mind of a sun-warmed wolf pup in the first spring of life. ART WOLFE

Charles Darwin was one of the first to note this gender dichotomy—males tend to mate whenever they can but females may pick and choose—though he was at a loss to account for it. But whatever the evolutionary "reason" for female choice, it has at least one important consequence. It gives animal mothers an extra measure of control over their reproductive fortunes. The biggest contribution that a mother makes to the success of her young may well lie in her choice of their father.

The world being what it is, a female's sexual choices are not always unfettered. A mother mouse, for example, may face particularly unpleasant alternatives. If she opts for one partner (we'll call him Tom), her offspring have a chance to live; if she decides on another (Jerry), they will surely die. In this scenario, Jerry is the dominant mouse in a meadow, where he is accepted as a breeding partner by the resident females. The pups that are born on his territory are his own, and he will not harm them. But if Jerry is ousted by Tom, the newcomer will slaughter all his predecessor's infants and try to initiate his own litters. This is a disaster for the females who have already invested time and energy in Jerry's youngsters.

Mammalian motherhood is always oriented toward the future.

Rather than suffer such a traumatic loss, pregnant female mice, lemmings and voles can cut their losses by reabsorbing their budding embryos. This response (called the "Bruce effect," after its discoverer, Hilda Bruce) occurs at the first scent of an invader. The pregnancy spontaneously ends. Then, with their ill-fated litters out of the way, the females mate with the new territory holder, perhaps aware that his litters are safe, at least while he is in power.

Mammalian motherhood is always oriented toward the future. Although some creatures (like butterflies) reproduce just once and die, most mammals produce young repeatedly throughout their lifetimes. If the current batch of youngsters is doomed, an efficient animal mother will dump them as soon as possible in order to conserve her energy for the next time round. For example, if a pregnant lynx suffers through an especially difficult winter, she may abort her fetuses rather than devote her scanty resources to producing weaklings. Scrawny, sickly kittens are not likely to thrive, either as juveniles or

Blessed with a favorable birth-season, this lynx kitten may eventually reward its parents by producing numerous descendants. Her success will depend on the abundance of prey in her lifetime, especially snowshoe hares. ALAN AND SANDY CAREY

as breeding adults. By sparing herself the burden of an ill-fated pregnancy, the mother has a chance to build up body reserves for the following season when, if all goes well, she will give birth to big, healthy youngsters. These infants, born under auspicious stars, will likely make her a grandmother many times over. By "choosing" not to breed when times are tough, an animal may ultimately multiply her descendants.

"To breed or not to breed" is the question—one that, for some mammals, is explicitly posed every year by the mother's reproductive system. Some female bats, for example, store their partner's sperm after mating and only proceed to conception if the times look good. A diverse assortment of animal mothers, including skunks, weasels, bears and armadillos, follow a slightly different strategy. Conception occurs at the time of mating, usually in the fall, but the embryo neither develops nor implants in the uterus. Months later, often in midwinter, the mother's body either proceeds with the pregnancy or opts out, depending on her food supply and physical condition. Since the mother has virtually no investment in the embryo before this decision point, "delayed implantation" provides a mechanism for low-cost abortions.

Female mammals are obviously not just baby-incubating machines, constantly set to On.

Female mammals are obviously not just baby-incubating machines, constantly set to On. Animals make physiological choices, based on sophisticated assessments of their present and future prospects, about when to breed and when to shut themselves down. (Nature, it seems, is pro-choice.) What's more, some mammals are apparently capable of influencing not only when they give birth but also, within limits, to whom. Specifically, they may have a "say" in determining the gender of their youngsters. Although the subject remains contentious, biologists are attracted to the idea that mammals (like insects) are able to manipulate the sex ratio of their offspring.

Evolutionary theory has it that a healthy, well-fed female mammal should produce more sons than daughters. In most mammalian societies, a few males do most of the breeding, and an ill-born male will never get his fair share of the action. But a big, bouncing baby boy that grows into a large, dominant male will likely sire dozens—or even

Although a female grizzly mates in the fall, her embryos do not "implant" in the womb for several weeks afterward. No more than a handful at birth, this cub was born during its mother's hibernation. LEONARD LEE RUE III

OVERLEAF A mountain lion kitten patiently submits to its mother's rough-tongued zeal for cleanliness. TOM AND PAT LEESON

hundreds—of offspring. By contrast, an equally well-nourished daughter cannot boost her reproductive output very much, because she is limited by the cycle of pregnancy and lactation. Thus, since sons benefit more than daughters from a head start in life, a mother in excellent condition should bias her reproductive output toward males. Conversely, a female that is struggling or stressed should rear extra daughters, since they are likely to produce normal numbers of offspring even without a privileged childhood.

Although the evidence is complex and contradictory, these principles apparently operate across a wide spectrum of mammalian species, from hamsters to mule deer and baboons to humpback whales. In some cases, the chance of producing a daughter or son seems to depend on when the parents mate. Among humans, for example, a couple is more likely to have a boy if they copulate three or four days before ovulation occurs, or a day or two afterward. Among golden hamsters, early matings result in more females, late ones in extra males. Alternatively, unequal sex ratios can result because some embryos fail to thrive or to implant—or even because the mother acts against them. Take the coypu, for example, a stout, aquatic rodent from South America that has been introduced to parts of the United States and Great Britain. When a young, well-fed female coypu becomes pregnant, she will carry her offspring to term if she has

A male mouse that is gestated between two brothers will likely grow up to be a gentle soul that takes a paternal interest in his offspring.

conceived either a large litter or a small one that consists mainly of male embryos. But if she is carrying a small, mainly female litter, she is likely to abort. The next time round (which for her comes very soon), she is almost certain to produce more offspring or more sons or both. Only females in superb condition, who have the potential to produce super-sexy sons, go to the trouble of making these adjustments.

From the point of view of an ecologist, the ratio of males to females in a rodent litter is important because it affects reproduction rates, population structures and other basic demographic variables. From the point of view of a coypu pup or a baby mouse, the impact is much more direct and personal. The number of brothers and sisters one has and the way they're arranged in the womb has a major formative effect on an individual's

For animals born in litters — like these month-old coyote pups — brothers and sisters are an ever-present social influence. ERWIN AND PEGGY BAUER

nature. A male mouse that is gestated between two brothers will likely grow up to be a gentle soul that takes a paternal interest in his offspring. Chances are, he will not be infanticidal. A female that develops in the same circumstances will mature late and produce relatively few young, presumably as a result of her early exposure to male hormones. As an adult, she will bear more sons than daughters, so her female offspring are also likely to gestate between brothers. They will therefore share the characteristics she acquired in the womb—a remarkable example of the nongenetic inheritance of a mother's attributes.

A fetus may develop in its mother's womb for two weeks or two years (from twelve days for a marsupial "cat" to more than twenty-two months for an elephant). Much as a caterpillar is transformed into a butterfly, so a blob of fetal cells is shaped and sculpted into a baby mammal. The plan for the transformation is set by the infant's genes, but finishing touches are added through the influence of littermates and especially the mother. In one laboratory experiment, a baby rat was taken from her mother too soon after birth and, as a result, became susceptible to stress ulcers. Sometime later, when she produced pups of her own, her pups turned out to suffer from the same problem. This difference—which persisted if the youngsters were raised by a foster mom—must have been caused by exposure to the mother's hormones *in utero*. In a second, similar experiment, a confident young female rat was subjected to a brief period of stress and thereafter became a timorous beast, who did her best to hide if she was put in an open field. When her offspring were born, they all shared her unadventurous nature—and her grandpups did, as well. Again, the effect persisted even when the young were raised by substitute mothers.

Ever since poor old Lamarck was discredited by the findings of Darwin and Mendel, everyone has agreed that animals cannot inherit their parents' acquired characteristics. (If your mother carries a gene for strong muscles, you can hope to inherit this attribute. But if she's a natural-born weakling who works out at the gym, you cannot expect to be born with her bulging biceps.) Yet it has recently become clear that because mammalian embryos develop in intimate contact with their mother, they can be shaped by her prior experience. Genetic change is slow and haphazard; maternal influence is immediate and focused. A female rat that narrowly escaped the talons of a hawk might later give birth to

For a Grant's zebra, the first rule of life is to stay close to mother's side. It's as simple as black and white. GLEN AND REBECCA GRAMBO

pups that were afraid to enter meadows. If predators were plentiful, her lineage would thrive, while those that lacked her cautionary experience would go forth boldly and die. Mothering helps free mammals from the rigid control of their genetic "hardware" and permits frequent, subtle changes to their "software" and lifestyle.

Although you won't find this sentiment celebrated on Mother's Day cards, mammalian motherhood is a powerful evolutionary force.

On land and in the seas, the contours of mammalian life are shaped by mothering. Here, an Australian sea lion pup follows the graceful sweep of its parent's body. JEFF FOOTT

OVERLEAF Oblivious to everything but warmth and rest, two red fox pups snooze in the entranceway to their den. DANIEL J. COX/NATURAL EXPOSURES

ONLY A MOTHER KNOWS
A MOTHER'S FONDNESS.

LADY MARY WORTLEY MONTAGU, LETTER TO A FRIEND, 1754

III | THAT'S MY BABY

THE IDEA THAT FEMALES are endowed with an innate "maternal instinct" is a venerable one. But the fact is that mammals are not all born with an insatiable yearning to care for young. A virgin female rat, for example, typically shows every sign of detesting pups. Forced into their presence, she draws away, closes her eyes and generally acts as if she is horrified by the mere fact of their existence. She may even try to bury them in bedding, in an attempt to keep their disagreeable odor away from her nose and whiskers. Yet when this same female becomes pregnant, she will find herself enamored of the little darlings—the very same infants whom, a week or two before, she had despised with her whole heart.

Biologist Ruth Ewer once witnessed a similar transformation in the attitude of a female

"Mother, do you have to do that in public?" An elk (or red deer) calf draws away as its mother uses her nose to confirm the identity of her infant. DANIEL J. COX/NATURAL EXPOSURES

OVERLEAF A two-month old cheetah kitten settles in to enjoy the benefits of motherly devotion. NORBERT ROSING

house cat toward one of her weaned kittens. Pregnant with a new litter, the mother cat acted as if she had grown to hate her half-grown son, whom she repelled with hissing and claws whenever he appeared. This went on for weeks. Then, just before she was ready to give birth, he happened to approach, perhaps expecting the worst, and instead found himself licked and caressed like the most lovable kitty on Earth. "In the brief space of half an hour he had metamorphosed from an undesirable, to be driven away at all costs, into an object of extreme maternal solicitude."

An animal's inclination to care for her young can be switched on and off by her hormones. In the lab, a virgin female rat with a taste for killing pups can be quickly transformed into an attentive caregiver. The simplest way is to give her injections of three chemicals: the female sex hormones estrogen and progesterone and a pregnancy hormone called prolactin. In the normal scheme of things, these substances are produced by the endocrine glands, the placenta and the fetus itself (making a covert bid for its mother's care). Under the influence of this elixir, a mother-to-be often begins to make preparations for the birth of her offspring by gathering nest material or starting work on her den. At the same time, she may develop

An animal's inclination to care for her young can be switched on and off by her hormones.

a passionate interest in her neighbor's young, even to the point of baby-snatching. A pregnant mouse, for example, may grab a stray pup, hold it down with her paws and groom it enthusiastically before letting it go. A female sheep may actually steal another ewe's lamb and forcibly keep the bleating mother at a distance. But when the kidnapper gives birth herself, her captive loses its charm, and she directs her maternal fervor toward her own newborn.

There is nothing especially tender about the act of giving birth. Yet surprisingly, the physical trauma of birthing turns out to be another important stimulus for maternal tenderness. The muscular rending and stretching that propel infants out into the world also send powerful signals coursing through the mother's nerves. These messages trigger changes in her brain, which in turn influence her hormones—and her behavior. Thus a ewe will not normally adopt an unfamiliar youngster. But if her cervix is manipulated to simulate giving

As her fawn prepares to take its first wobbly steps, a female deer consumes a delicious repast of hormone-rich afterbirth. ERWIN AND PEGGY BAUER

birth, she is likely to accept any lamb that is presented to her.

The physical sensations of parturition are just the first stage in the sensory extravaganza of birthing. As each infant emerges from the vagina, an animal mother is treated to an array of pleasing tastes and scents. Eagerly, she grasps the newborn with her paws, draws it toward her mouth and begins to lick it with gusto. In the process, she not only washes off amniotic fluid and removes the birth membranes, she also stimulates the nerves that control the infant's first intake of breath. (Sometimes a mother goat becomes so intent on licking that she totally frustrates her youngster's attempts to stand or to nurse. Every time it tries to rise, she pushes it down with her foot. If, conversely, she fails to lick it at all, it is likely to lie down and die.) Finally, to complete her postpartum feast, the mother eagerly eats the afterbirth. Although her willingness to consume this mess wanes after she's given birth, virtually every mammalian mother experiences a momentary enthusiasm for eating gooey membranes—with one fortunate exception. Indeed, one wag has suggested that our species be defined "as the primate that does not normally eat the placenta."

As the cumulative effect of all these experiences, the female enters what biologists call the "maternal state," which renders her willing and able to provide care for infants. In some species, this is a generalized response to any and all youngsters. A mother rat, for example, will cross an electrified grid to rescue young infants, regardless of whether they are her own or someone else's. In one experiment, a rat brought in a total of fifty-eight youngsters and would have gone after even more if the scientists hadn't run out of pups for her to carry home. In other trials, rats have been known to retrieve mice, rabbits, chicks and even kittens in a superabundance of maternal zeal.

As far as we can tell, many species of rodents and some carnivores (including house cats) cannot recognize their own offspring. In the laboratory, these animals will care for any infant they are offered. But in nature, they seldom become confused, because their young are kept sequestered in private dens or in secluded corners of the forest. Any infant that's in the right place is likely to have the right parentage. Mammals that mix and mingle, on the other hand, generally have a better sense of who's who. A prairie gopher (or Richardson's ground squirrel) will nurse any pup that is dropped down her nest hole;

Raising a complaint that would touch the hardest heart, this wolf pup
is likely to attract the care of all the adults in its pack. RICK MCINTYRE

but as soon as the youngsters come out to play with their age-mates in the colony, she refuses to accept any except those she has raised. Unable to identify her youngsters when it was unnecessary, she quickly learns to recognize them by scent, sight and voice when it becomes important for her to do so.

For some species of mammals, bonding with baby—getting to know one's own off-spring as an individual—matters from the moment of birth. A Mexican free-tailed bat, for example, bears her pup in a bustling nursery cave. When she goes off to feed, she leaves her infant hanging from the rocks, cheek by jowl with ten thou-sand other almost-identical youngsters. There seems little hope she will ever see it again, one among so many thousands. Indeed, for many years, scientists believed that returning females simply permitted themselves to be suckled by any infant that managed to grasp hold of a nipple. But DNA studies have shown that a mother bat does locate and nurse her own pup, even in this throng, on well over 80 per cent of her trips home. She is assisted in this feat by a faint glandular scent with which she marks her pup and by its eager response to her homecoming vocal-izations. "It's me, Mom. Over here."

In most ways that matter, women are remarkably unlike ewes.

Nobody knows exactly when and how bats form this attachment to their infants. Does the process take time? Does it ever fail? But we do know something about a similar process in sheep and goats. Sheep, for instance, live in tight flocks that offer plenty of scope for confusion and accidental baby-swaps. To guard against this possibility, ewes experience a period of heightened awareness in the first few hours after giving birth, during which they are exquisitely sensitive to the taste and smell of their newborns. In as little as ten minutes of licking and sniffing, a mother sheep memorizes the unique olfactory signature of her youngster. Thereafter, she will accept no other; indeed, she violently repels any pre-tenders. But if her lamb is taken from her at birth and kept away for a few hours, the window of sensitivity closes and she treats it like a total stranger. The moment has been lost and the lamb abandoned.

In most ways that matter, women are remarkably unlike ewes. Yet for the last twenty-five years, the mother-infant bonding of sheep has been widely accepted as an appropriate model for humans. According to scholar Diane E. Eyer, this "craze" was born in the 1970s, as the offspring of bad science and rapid social change. Despite its dubious parentage, the theory flourished because, on the one hand, it appealed to social conservatives, who wanted women to stay at home. At the same time, the idea met the needs of working mothers, who liked the thought that parent-child attunement could be assured by a little quality time immediately after birth. Ever since, experts have solemnly advised us that the first hours or days of life are crucially important to the mother-infant bond, as if people, like sheep, had a tightly defined sensitive period. Yet there is no evidence that this is true.

Similarly, many psychologists stress the critical importance of a secure relationship between baby and its "primary caregiver" (a.k.a. "mother"), as if human childcare were inevitably an isolated, one-on-one project—one lamb, one ewe—rather than a familial or communal undertaking. The evidence on this point is, at best, ambiguous, as competing studies conclude that multiple caregivers are, or are not, beneficial to very young children. Perhaps in the end it will turn out that humans are less like sheep and more like wolves, lions, elephants and other social mammals, among whom infants form bonds not only with their mothers but also with their sisters, aunts, grandmothers and, sometimes, their brothers, uncles and dads.

IV | MOTHERHOOD
ISSUES

BABY MAMMALS HAVE THE POWER to turn adult humans into simpering idiots. "Kitchy gooey little wumwums, let me rub your little tumtums," we trill at the kitties in their basket. The problem is, they're just *so* cute, and we, as a species, have a weakness for cuteness. Show us a small form with short legs, an overly large head and big, round eyes, and we will fall for it in an instant. Could be a baby seal, could be a teddy bear. It doesn't really matter—we will find it attractive. If its movements are clumsy and clownish, like those of a two-year-old child, so much the better. In fact, anything that reminds us, however vaguely, of a human infant or toddler makes an instant appeal for our affection.

And humans are not the only mammals with a soft spot for the young. Given the

As Konrad Lorenz was one of the first to point out, humans have an innate weakness for cute infants. Babies also seem to have a powerful appeal for some other mammals, especially primates like the olive baboon. ART WOLFE

choice between looking at pictures of baby monkeys and older juveniles, female rhesus monkeys prefer to gaze at the little ones. When an infant is born into a monkey colony, the females all crowd round, just like humans at a baby shower, hoping for a chance to touch or hold the newcomer. There is something about young mammals—the way they look, sound and smell—that can be powerfully attractive to their potential caregivers. Even virgin female rats, which normally detest young pups, become willing to provide care if kept in a cage with them for a week or so. In fact, sustained exposure to the mere *odor* of pups can be enough to bring about this transformation. After a week bathed in the scent of a litter of young, the most antimaternal of rats finds herself overcome by an irresistible desire to groom and brood them. Some animals—wolves, elephants, various kinds of monkeys—have even been known to produce milk for adoptees.

When it comes to assuring the care of baby mammals, evolution has taken no chances. First, the pregnant female is served a hormonal cocktail that puts her in the mood for motherhood. Then she is presented with an infant that has been perfected over millions of years for the precise purpose of eliciting her devotion. In the dry language of evolutionary biology, infant mammals are said to be "efficient releasers of nurturent behavior." A friend of mine, reflecting on how she had avoided infanticide in the first, sleepless months of her young son's life, made the same point more wryly. "Cuteness has survival value," she said; and she was exactly right.

Though the characteristics that warm a mother's heart may be very different for a person than for a rat, the appeal of infants and their ability to "turn on" maternal care seem to be widespread among mammals. But what a mother is prepared to do as a result of this attraction is another matter. By human standards, the females of some species are downright negligent. One thinks, for example, of the tree shrew, a tiny, twitchy creature that bears her pups in a burrow and then leaves them alone for up to forty-eight hours. When she finally returns, she squats over the mouth of the nest and squirts milk into their waiting mouths for all of ten minutes; then away she speeds for another day or two on her own. During her brief appearances, she does not groom, brood, turn or otherwise attend her infants.

Tree shrew pups are sturdy little things, well adapted to cope with absentee mothering. But most newborns are both more dependent and more demanding. Even fawns, which are ready to take their first steps within minutes of birth, are dependent on their mother for basic life support. Like most baby mammals, they cannot even excrete without parental help. To get them to "go," the mother must massage their backsides with her tongue. Then, to protect them from detection by predators, she may eat their waste products. (And we complain about changing diapers!) For some animals, this intimate attention apparently has a lifelong impact. A male rat that is not licked enough as a pup will be slow to ejaculate when he mates as a grown-up.

For a newborn mammal, mothering makes the difference between life and death. But it also has other, remarkably subtle effects on infant development. If a newborn gets too hot, it will likely die of dehydration. An attentive mother therefore provides protection, perhaps by hiding her babies in cool shade (in the case of a giraffe) or moistening them with her dampened fur (in the case of a polecat). If, on the other hand, the thermometer falls, a mother rat may warm her infants with her body heat, gauging her visits so that the babies stay at precisely the right temperature. Her judgment must be exact. If young rats are experimentally removed from their nest and cooled to room temperature—a drop of just three degrees—the growth of their brains, internal organs and skeletons slows down dramatically. By timing her attendance at the nest, a mother rat controls her pups' temperature and thus actually determines the rate at which they mature.

When it comes to assuring the care of baby mammals, evolution has taken no chances.

Mothering even affects the heart rate of the infant. From experiments again with rats (those most probed and prodded of laboratory subjects), it appears that the heartbeat of the infant is regulated by the rate at which the mother provides it with food. When pups are separated from their mothers, their pulse slows drastically. But if these infants are then fed by stomach tube, their heart rates rise and fall delicately, depending on the amount of milk they are given. Just how this occurs remains mysterious (though presumably information passes from the stomach to the brain and thence to the heart). In some way that is

OVERLEAF Good parenting does not always require constant attention. Lying still and almost scentless, this pronghorn calf provides few clues to predators and can safely be left to hide between feedings. DENVER A. BRYAN

even less well understood, the presence of the mother also determines the level of growth hormones secreted by her infants. If a mother rat is absent, even for a few minutes, the hormone levels in the pups' bodies drop; when she comes back, they quickly return to normal. This regulation is not achieved through changes in temperature or nutrition but through some as yet unidentified aspect of the relationship between mother and infant.

The rough-and-tumble of family life also helps to determine the "mood" of the infant. When a nice calm baby rat is taken from its mother, it soon becomes nervous and hyper-active. Even if the pup has everything it needs—warmth, food and company—something seems to be missing. The most likely candidate is the mother's touch, which has a calming effect on many young mammals. In a set of classic (if cruel) experiments with rhesus monkeys, infants were removed from their mothers and raised on cloth-covered dummies, or "surrogates." As one might expect, the babies who suffered this gross deprivation grew up to be social misfits. Oddly, the worst of their abnormalities could be prevented simply by mounting the dummies on wires. This way, the surrogates swayed when the infants clung to them, creating the illu-sion that their "mothers" were handling them. This comfortable jostling by their caregivers somehow helped them prepare for the give-and-take of the adult social world.

Infants are exclusively, obsessively tuned to their mother's wavelength.

If mothers are predisposed to find their infants cute, infants are inclined to find their mothers impressive. Everything a mammalian mother does, however unassuming, has the potential to be received, interpreted and amplified by her offspring. Infants are exclusively, obsessively tuned to their mother's wavelength. From her, they acquire the basic rhythms of life. Unawares, they learn her parenting style (attentive or rejecting, anxious or calm) and acquire the aptitude for sexual and social behavior in adult life. Almost as sensitive to their mother as they were before birth, young mammals continue to be shaped by her unique nature and experience.

Given all this, it is no great surprise that young mammals do not like to be separated from their mothers. From rats to monkeys, the response is much the same. The bereaved infant squeaks and squawks as if in pain and runs around aimlessly. It may even show signs of depression, such as decreased pulse, lowered body temperature and inability to sleep. Mothers, however, may seem remarkably unperturbed about the disappearance or even the death of an infant. A tree shrew, on one of her brief home visits, will search for her litter for a good two minutes; if she doesn't find them in that time, she will give up and never return. A female deer or moose will risk her life to battle a coyote or wolf, but if the predator grabs her youngster, she may turn and walk away as if nothing had happened. Is she indifferent or in despair?

We cannot know how animals feel about one another. But at times their actions invite us to draw conclusions. When a mother elephant carries her dead calf on her tusks for days on end, putting it down only to eat and drink, we are tempted to think of grief. When Scarlet the cat makes five separate trips into a burning house to rescue her month-old kittens, we suspect that we know something about her motives. And when a monkey reaches out to stroke her sleeping child so gently it does not wake, we know that we are seeing something familiar. This may not be love as humans experience it, but surely it must be elephant love, cat love, monkey love—variations on the theme of mammalian motherhood.

V | LIQUID ASSETS

MILK IS NATURE'S PERFECT FOOD, we're told, but it would be more accurate to recast this statement in the plural. Mammalian milk is not one food but many, each of them true to an ancestral recipe and suited to the needs of a particular species. If there were connoisseurs of milk, as there are of wine, they would be able to distinguish platypus milk from porpoise, skunk from seal, simply by comparing the smell, taste and texture of the competing vintages. "Ah, blue whale, unmistakable—note that fine fishy bouquet, with just a hint of liver. Rather hearty taste, like Milk of Magnesia, and the typical oily feel. Yes, I'd say, a very good year in the North Atlantic."

Milks are all made from the same basic ingredients (minerals, proteins, sugars and

A mother capybara stands stoically as a horde of hungry pups tugs at her nipples. Some rodents are born with special teeth that help them to grab their mother's teats. ART WOLFE

fats), combined in varying proportions. The perfect balance for any given species depends on the dietary requirements of the infant—very different for a wallaby, say, than for a walrus. But the nutritional needs of the mother also enter into the equation. A mother seal, for example, feeds in the sea but must haul out on land or ice to give birth and to nurse her pup. As long as she stays around the whelping grounds, she gets little or nothing to eat. The moment she leaves, she risks losing her pup in the crush of the colony. What to do?

Evolution has responded to this dilemma by brewing a power-house milk—at 50 to 60 per cent fat, it is almost twice as rich as whipping cream. Liberally provisioned with this luxurious beverage, a seal pup grows up fast, rapidly doubling and then trebling its natal weight. By the time it is weaned—within *four days* to four weeks, depending on the species—the pup is a chubby little blub-berball, literally able to live off its fat when its mother abruptly leaves. Every gram that Junior has gained has been its mother's loss, and her body weight will have been reduced by 40 to 60 per cent during this brief period. Pressed by the urgent hunger that all nursing mothers share, she abandons her pup and heads out to sea in search of a decent meal.

Keeping a youngster stuffed with milk is always costly.

Although few mammals pay such a high price for nursing, keeping a youngster stuffed with milk is always costly. (On average, a breast-feeding woman loses about three kilograms, or eight pounds, of fat—nature's own postpartum weight-loss plan.) In addition to the direct energy drain on her body, a nursing mother may face other challenges. A lactating wolf or cheetah is tied to her den and may have to commute long, wearying distances to her hunting grounds. A grazing animal, such as a wild sheep, may shift to poor-quality pasture if it permits her to keep her young safe from predators. As long as her lambs are suckling, she must stay with them and somehow manage to get by on thin rations. These constraints add to the stress of nursing and increase the possibility that the mother will have to draw on her own tissues—including her skeleton—to keep up the flow of nutrients to her infants.

Milk production has another hidden cost. It makes some females markedly more aggressive. When an infant grasps a teat, the sucking stimulation causes chemical changes in the mother's brain. Under the influence of these mood-altering secretions, a mild-mannered female may be transformed into an avenging superhero. Anyone who threatens her young, or even gets too close, can expect violent retribution. Far from being the preserve of testosterone-pumped males, aggression turns out to be a motherly trait in a wide range of mammals, including mice, squirrels, rabbits, cats, sheep and baboons. Just as people are wise to give a wide berth to a bear with cubs, even a grizzly must respect a moose defending her calves. Made brave—even reckless—by lactation, an animal runs the risk of being injured or killed when she confronts her foes. As a result, nursing mothers are more likely to die than nonnursing females.

In one way and another, females go to the wall because of milk. So you'd expect them to be choosy about who gets to drink this precious liquid—and most of the time they are. In the first place, they try to make sure that it goes to their own offspring. Animals like mice, which may not be able to identify their own pups, restrict their nursing to their home nests. Others, like sheep and seals, which bond with their young, are vigilant to ensure that every drop goes to them. If a young stranger tries to butt in, the mother repels it with force. Milk is a mother's investment in the future, and it is in her best interests to keep it in the family.

But the mammalian definition of "family" is not static. Even a one-and-only animal like a sheep is sometimes called upon to enlarge her understanding. If, for example, her own lamb dies, a ewe may adopt an orphaned nephew or niece and permit it to suckle as if it were her own. Female lions, which live in tight-knit kinship groups, nurse each other's young almost as a matter of course.

Black-tailed prairie dogs are more mercurial. While prairie dog pups are still too young to venture above ground, neighboring females nip into their burrows and kill them. Since all the animals in the colony are related, this amounts to a slaughter of their own kith and kin. Thirty per cent of all litters are hit by assassins. But when the surviving pups emerge from their dens, they are welcomed with open arms, and the neighbors take them to their breasts (or at least to their teats). Almost three-quarters of emergent pups receive milk from the same females who earlier would have murdered them.

OVERLEAF A human baby takes about six months to double its birth weight. Fed on its mother's double-rich cream, a harp seal accomplishes the same goal in five days. NORBERT ROSING

The reason for this bizarre turnaround remains obscure, but it may have something to do with a change in the "value" of the pups. Early in the season, when browse is scarce, those juicy pink little morsels may be most useful as food. Later, when they come above ground, they form a living shield for one's own vulnerable brood. If a predator swoops over a crowd of pups, there's a good chance that the one it grabs will belong to someone else. Like the witch in "Hansel and Gretel," who lures children with treats, the prairie dog draws pups around her with a "generous" offer of milk.

Although we wreath "nursing moms" with ribbons and pink lace, lactation is often surprisingly tough and strategic. Think, for example, of a goat that gives birth to twin kids, one vigorous, the other wobbly. Should she abandon the weakling and save her milk for the stronger kid? Or should she help the runt build up its strength by giving it extra sustenance? Somehow, animals are able to choose between such difficult options. If the goat decides to favor the needy kid, she will not be deterred or distracted by the high-pitched complaints of its healthy sib.

A nursing mother can also discriminate among her offspring on the basis of their sex. A male that has a chance to become a superstud will likely be provisioned with superabundant milk. The mother accomplishes this by letting her son nurse more often and for longer than she would a daughter. Highly polygynous mammals, such as red deer and elephant seals, are known to allocate their resources in exactly this way. Some species, however, favor females. Rhesus monkeys live in matrilineal clans that increase in size as daughters are born to them. (Daughters remain in their birth groups; sons leave to join other troops.) As the clan enlarges, the status and success of its members rise with each new addition. A daughter is, therefore, a pearl of great price, well worth the extra milk and care that are lavished upon her.

At the same time that an animal attempts to make the most of her current batch of young, she must also keep something in reserve for those that will be born in the future. She cannot give her all to her present offspring if it means she will not have the resources to produce healthy young in the following year. Thus, in a bad spring, when pastures are poor and birthing is delayed, a flock of Dall's sheep may allow their lambs to nurse more

OVERLEAF Adult koalas eat strong-tasting eucalyptus leaves, which infants cannot digest. As youngsters are weaned, they are switched to a diet of detoxified leaves, in the form of special droppings, which they lick from their mother's anus. ERWIN AND PEGGY BAUER

than usual for a time and then wean them early. The lambs will complain loudly about this decision, but the mothers have good reason to be insistent. Having given these youngsters the best start they can, they need a chance to recover their strength before the next breeding season.

By managing lactation, a mother gains a measure of control over her reproductive prospects. She does this not only by regulating her physical condition but also by directly adjusting her fertility. Among mammals in general, nursing has a contraceptive effect. For Japanese macaque monkeys, to cite a typical case, a female's chance of becoming pregnant drops by a third while she is feeding an infant. To compensate for this effect, a mother that normally suckles her infant on demand puts it on a schedule by enforcing longer breaks between nursing bouts during the mating season. This simple change alters her hormones, with the result that she becomes more likely to conceive. A mother in poor condition might let her baby nurse at will in an attempt to take a break from her hectic reproductive career.

In contrast to many smaller mammals, which breed at a hectic rate,
a polar bear gives birth to one or two cubs, which accompany her for
about two years after weaning. NORBERT ROSING

> IT IS A WISE FATHER THAT
> KNOWS HIS OWN CHILD.
>
> WILLIAM SHAKESPEARE, *THE MERCHANT OF VENICE*, 1600

VI | WHAT ABOUT DAD?

AS ANYONE WHO HAS CARED FOR TODDLERS will readily attest, trying to meet the needs of youngsters can run you ragged. And if humans feel this challenge, even with condoms and pills, what must it be like for the poor, technologically deprived animals? Female mammals often get caught in a reproductive spin, as birth follows birth in rapid succession. A coyote, for example, bears up to nineteen pups each spring. By the time they are half grown, she finds herself pregnant again. Worse yet, a female cottontail may have three litters in a year, for a total annual production of two dozen bunnies. It doesn't bear contemplating.

There is one obvious question that begs to be asked. With this much work to be done,

Male lions are supremely at ease with cubs born on their home territories. Alien young, by contrast, often fall prey to the males' strong jaws.
JOHNNY JOHNSON

OVERLEAF Despite its good-natured appeal, this elephant seal pup will never know a father's love. WAYNE LYNCH

where are all the dads? The typical mammalian family is raised by the mother alone, with no visible assistance from the father. This situation holds for more than 90 per cent of mammalian genera, in which paternal care has never been witnessed. While the mother looks after the youngsters, dad is off in a world of his own, preoccupied with such macho concerns as social status and territorial defense. At best, his actions have an indirect impact on the fortunes of his young. If he competes with other males for the right to breed, his infants reap the benefits of his genetic quality. If he maintains a territory for himself and his mate (or mates), his progeny enjoy the advantages of peace and plenty. But clean a dirty bottom or collect bedding for the nest? You might as well forget it.

Male animals have two good reasons for staying clear of their young. One is that they are poorly equipped to take care of them. A male cannot become pregnant and hence has nothing much to offer during gestation. When it comes to lactation, he's not much better off. Although his breasts are physiologically capable of secreting milk, he does not normally produce the hormones that are needed to make them work. (One possible exception is a rare rain forest bat from the Krau Game Reserve in Malaysia. Of twenty mature males that were examined in recent surveys, more than half were found to be lactating. No one knows, however, if they actually fed pups.)

Male animals have two good reasons for staying clear of their young.

Unless a male can find a way to boost the survival of his young, he is simply wasting his time by hanging around home. Far better, from his point of view, to roam the wide world on a constant quest for females that will accept his sperm. But males are not always bound by this knightly code of behavior. When their care is actually needed, some of them are both willing and able to provide it. This is the case, for example, with the humble meadow vole. As long as the weather is warm, mother voles manage quite well alone, and fathers do not usually stay with their litters. But come autumn, when the temperature drops, females can no longer cope on their own. Whenever the mother leaves her nest, her pups are threatened by cold. Happily, father may fill the gap by moving in with the brood.

Male wolves—including fathers, uncles, older brothers and others—share in all the duties of infant care except for nursing. This can include occasional service as a chew toy. TOM AND PAT LEESON

Whether or not a male vole assists at the nest depends, in part, on his past relationship with his own father. Males are more nurturing if they were raised by both parents. While some of the influence may be genetic ("like father, like son"), paternal care may also be partially learned. This conclusion is strongly suggested by an experiment in which male meadow vole pups (from a species in which father care is seasonal, at most) were fostered by white-footed mice (among which two-parent families are usual). Voles that were raised by sensitive New Age mice were more likely to help with their own pups than they would have been otherwise.

Paternal care is the road less traveled by mammals. Yet there is a small, disparate group of species—including a few rodents, certain carnivores and many primates—among which fathers are natural-born caregivers. From white-footed mice to wolves and tamarins, these animals all tend to be strongly monogamous. A major factor that prevents males from caring for young is that they cannot identify their own daughters and sons. Even if they remember where they put their sperm, they cannot be certain that someone else's didn't hit home first. Since fertilization is hidden from sight by the female body, the typical male is paralyzed by paternal uncertainty. Rather than risk putting his energy into somebody else's offspring, he takes the manly way out and does nothing.

A monogamous male, on the other hand, has reasonable grounds to assume that any pup born to his mate is his alone. The more confidence a male has that an infant belongs to him, the more likely he is to settle down and care for it. For instance, a male house mouse does not usually like young pups; in fact, his first impulse may be to kill them. If a typical bloodthirsty male is housed alone with a mate, he will continue to murder stray infants that are dropped into the cage. But one day, suddenly, his character will be reformed, and instead of attacking pups, he will start to cuddle them. This stunning metamorphosis (*Mr. Hyde Meets Mr. Mom*) occurs just before his partner gives birth to what can only be his litter of pups. Ever since the pair first mated, about three weeks before, his body has literally been counting the day-night cycles and timing his transformation into a model father.

Although little is known about the chemical basis of this conversion experience, we have more insight into the biological foundation of fatherhood in another rodent species. The California (deer) mouse is a cute little round-eared creature that always breeds in monogamous pairs. The father is involved with his infants from the moment of birth, picking up each in turn, licking it dry and warming it with his body. As the youngsters mature, he devotes himself to their care by sharing in all the nursery chores except for lactation. But his primary commitment is not really so much to his pups as it is to their mother, with whom he has an exclusive sexual bond. The presence of the female is the male's best guarantee that he is also in the presence of his own progeny.

The more confidence a male has that an infant belongs to him, the more likely he is to settle down and care for it.

For a male California mouse, the force that maintains his family values is the smell of his partner's urine. In one telling experiment, a mated pair was housed in a high-rise cage, with the male on the ground floor and the female in the attic. As long as her excreta showered gently down on his head, he retained his desire to care for infants. If the cascade was shut off (or another female's urine was substituted), his impulse for fatherhood quickly faded. Through his commitment to his partner's pee, if not to her person, the male mouse was able to ensure that his efforts would be directed toward his own progeny.

Among California mice, the male's participation is critical to the survival of his pups. Beset by cold rains and infanticidal neighbors, his mate has little chance of success as a single mother. In general, this is exactly why two-parent care has evolved, whether among mice, monkeys or humans. When one parent's efforts will not readily suffice to keep the youngsters alive, evolution calls up the reserves. A breeding stud is refashioned into a gentle caregiver.

Of all the mammals, none have adopted this strategy with greater effect than our own order, the primates. Like human infants, young monkeys and apes demand intensive attention for extended periods, sometimes well into adolescence. It's often too much for a mother to manage single-handed. So it's not surprising to discover that fatherly care has been noted in 40 per cent of primate genera and that monogamy is also quite common.

While some male primates ignore or attack infants (depending on their species and their dispositions), many others find babies irresistibly attractive. Thus, a newborn monkey may be welcomed into the world by a group of excited males, which cluster round eagerly in the hopes of handling it. As the youngster grows older, the males may engage it in play, initiate "social chatter" or hold it upright by the hands as if teaching it to walk. Should the infant's mother die, the little orphan may be adopted by one of its adult male companions.

Male primates sometimes have quirky reasons for caring for juveniles. In some species (like the Barbary macaque), a baby is a badge of peace that can be carried around to defuse confrontations with rival males. In others (like the Hamadryas baboon), adult males adopt infant females and rear them to adulthood as a way of acquiring sexual partners. But there are also straightforward cases of paternal nurturance. Marmosets and tamarins are small, soft-furred monkeys that live in Central and South America. Unlike most other primates, which generally have single births, these New World monkeys make a practice of bearing twins. Raising them is impossible unless father assists; in fact, the combined efforts of the entire family connection (both parents and older siblings) are often needed. Not only does the male help at the birth, he subsequently carries the infants—at a combined weight that soon nearly equals his own—all day, every day, except when they're being nursed. If the mother wants to take a turn, he will likely turn her down. Her job is to forage and produce milk; he and the rest of the family take care of everything else.

When a male tamarin approaches a female for sex, he does not try to seduce his mate with chocolates or roses. Instead, he is likely to show up carrying an infant. The females have a weakness for males that are likely to make good dads—a taste that many women may recognize in themselves.

In some troops of Japanese macaque monkeys, adult females look after the newborns and infants, while the males provide companionship to yearlings. ART WOLFE

OVERLEAF Among common marmosets and other New World monkeys, females rarely get a chance to carry their infants. This devoted caregiver is almost certainly the father or some other member of the extended family. ERWIN AND PEGGY BAUER

THERE IS A TIME TO CARE
AND A TIME TO KILL.

QOHELETH'S BOOK 3:3

VII | HONEY, I ATE THE KIDS

PARENTAL CARE IS ABSOLUTELY ESSENTIAL to mammals, as basic as eating or sex. So you might expect that the desire to nurture infants would be an infallible urge, ingrained in the psyche of each and every potential caregiver. Instead, adults of many species have been known to harm their young, whether through starvation, assault, rape or outright slaughter. Abuse and infanticide are both normal and perverse—the dark side of mammalian parental behavior.

The root of the problem is the age-old conflict between the generations. What is in the best interests of the infant is not always equally advantageous for its caregiver. Every youngster that is born wants to live and thrive, but its cold-hearted parent(s) may decree

When a new group of male lions sweeps into a territory, virtually all the young cubs are slaughtered and older youngsters are forced to flee. This happens routinely, about every two years. ART WOLFE

otherwise. Seen with the cruel gaze of evolution, a baby animal is just a means to an end: it represents a potential for future reproduction. A successful animal mother discriminates amongst her young and invests her energy where she will get the biggest bang for her buck. In other words, she takes good care of youngsters that seem likely to reward her with numerous grandchildren.

The rest she may dispatch without any apparent qualms. For example, a female that gives birth to more offspring than she can rear will quickly rid herself of the surplus. An ibex that bears triplets instead of twins leaves one of them to die. A hamster or mouse with too many pups culls her litter and either eats the corpses herself or feeds them to their surviving brothers and sisters. If an animal is faced with the opposite problem—a litter that is too small—it may resort to similarly fatal options. Thus, a lion or a grizzly that has lost all but one cub may well abandon it in order to speed herself into breeding condition. Females of many species also desert young that are at a disadvantage due to overcrowding, lack of food or a shortage of caregivers. A California mouse that loses her mate (and valued co-parent) may respond by cannibalizing her entire litter.

If females are sometimes driven to kill their own young, they may feel even freer about disposing of other mothers' offspring. Among rhesus monkeys, the harassment begins before birth in assaults on pregnant females that can cause them to abort. Amazingly, the worst violence is directed selectively at monkeys that are carrying female embryos. Nobody knows how the attackers tell the sex of the unborn young (by the smell of the mothers' urine?), nor why they push their assaults to such a punishing conclusion. One possible explanation is that a female (but not a male) will join her mother's troop and compete for food and status with other members of the group. Since an ounce of prevention is worth a pound of cure, the neighbors attack the problem child before she can appear.

In most other instances, baby-killers are not concerned about their victims' gender. To a female ground squirrel, any and all of the neighbors' pups look equally good—when dead. Although colony members are related (mothers, sisters, aunts), their depredations on each other's burrows are the principal cause of infant death in most populations. Again, the reasons for their murderous tastes remain obscure, but it could be that killing pups in the den nips a problem in the bud. If the youngsters were allowed to mature and come above ground, they might manage to steal milk and care from their female neighbors. What simpler way to prevent this than by killing them as infants?

Competition between close relatives can also be the grounds for infanticide among wolves. Ordinarily, a wolf pack includes one mated pair, which are the parents of most other group members. The dominant animals try to prevent the others from breeding by harrying and harassing them throughout the mating season. If one of the subordinate females does manage to give birth, her mother will sniff and lick her pups as if to welcome them. Then she may calmly bite them until they are dead. Not only does this free her from helping to nurse the pups (which sometimes happens instead), it also frees her daughter to help at her mother's den. In this way, the dominant wolf is able to ensure that the resources of the entire pack are devoted to her litter.

By killing another male's progeny, an animal may be able to create his own reproductive opportunities.

Infanticide isn't pretty, but it is "motherly"—one of the strategies an animal can use to improve the survival prospects of her offspring. Males sometimes kill for much the same reason, that is, to give a competitive edge to their own descendants. What happens among lions is in many ways typical. Female lions live in female-based groups, or prides, and mate with the resident males in their area. As long as these males hold sway, the females' cubs are safe, because male lions do not kill young on their own territories. But after two or three years, these males fall to defeat and are forcibly supplanted by a rival group. The new arrivals establish themselves by slaughtering all the young cubs and driving off any older juveniles. The females, who up until now have resisted the takeover, quickly shift their allegiance to the new regime. When they come into breeding condition—within months of their loss—they permit the usurpers to father their next round of infants.

By killing another male's progeny, an animal may be able to create his own reproductive opportunities. Infanticide on this plan is committed not only by lions but also by rodents, wild horses, tigers, leopards, cougars, grizzlies, apes and monkeys. Although it's

OVERLEAF Sparring tiger cubs are vigorous and fierce, but they are still no match for a marauding adult tom bent on murder. Infanticide is known or suspected to occur among tigers, leopards and cougars. NORBERT ROSING

distasteful to humans, it is at least understandable. The same cannot be said for the wastage of life that sometimes occurs among seals, sea lions and walruses. For these animals, infants seem to be mere victims of circumstance. Difficulties arise whenever a herd pulls out on land, in a moody, undisciplined mob that includes adults of both sexes. The worst offenders are the huge, aggressive males, which throw their enormous bulk around as they contest for space and sex. In the general riot, pups are trampled and squashed. When a herd of walruses vacated one "resting" site, they left 119 dead, many of which were calves.

Calves and pups also suffer sexual abuse. Among pinnipeds, mating occurs immediately after the pups are born, right on the crowded birthing grounds. When the males strive with each other for a chance to breed, it's as if a gang fight had broken out in a nursery. Like infants in any war zone, pups often are killed, hurt or separated from their mothers. They may also be raped by pumped-up, pubescent males that have been denied access to the females. These assaults, which may be directed against either sex, are frequently accompanied by fatal bites to the neck.

Adult females are not blameless in this slaughter of innocents. Pups that lose their mothers in the confusion usually become permanent orphans, reduced to sneaking milk from strangers. These small crimes are often punishable by death, as offended females repel the little thieves with violence. Sometimes several adults join in the frenzy of death and compete to bite, shake and toss their helpless victims. Some seals, on the other hand, let the orphans nurse, but even this doesn't always help. A female may adopt several pups—more than she can support—with the result that most or all of them ultimately starve. Perhaps, instead of helping the pups, she is really helping herself, since suckling may be necessary to bring her into breeding condition. Is this caregiving or exploitation?

The same question can be asked about the "help" that is provided by some young monkeys and apes. Adolescent females (and many males) can't seem to keep their fingers off a newborn babe. They want to hold it, groom it, carry it around. Sometimes their services really are useful, as, for example, when they rescue a baby that has gone too far out on a limb or keep an eye on it while its mother feeds unencumbered. But sometimes they seem careless and inept. It's just not helpful to lose interest and leave an infant alone, or to

A sea lion pup that strays away from its mom runs a risk of trampling, assault, starvation, rape—or all of the above. JEFF FOOTT

drop it from a tree, or to carry it by one leg so that it thumps along the ground. Yet baby-sitting monkeys and apes make all these mistakes, which seem to be the result of inexperience. By practicing on (and at the expense of) other animals' young, they gradually become reasonably well schooled as parents.

For animals as for humans, parents are made, not born. Although skills are acquired with practice, the groundwork for parenting is actually laid down during infancy, in the interactions between an individual and her (or his) caregivers. If a female monkey is raised by a calm, tolerant mom, she will grow up to display much the same mothering style. If, on the other hand, her mother is jumpy and cross, she picks up this fretful disposition. Almost anything her infant does gives her cause for alarm, and she responds with vigorous nips and swats.

For animals as for humans, parents are made, not born.

Worse yet, a baby monkey that suffers the traumatic loss of her mother is almost certain to become an abusive parent. (This is true both in the laboratory and in the wild.) Anxious and overprotective, she will be easily overwhelmed by the inevitable small crises of infant care—a baby that won't stop crying or that refuses to do what she wants. The best and warmest of mothers when things are going well, she will strike out in panic whenever she's overstressed. In the end, her baby may be wounded or killed by excessive discipline. Clearly not adaptive in any sense of the word, these tragedies remind us that an unhappy childhood can cast a long shadow across the lives of both animals and humans.

Amid the crush and chaos of their breeding grounds, two female northern fur seals squabble over an infant. Behind them looms the intimidating form of a huge male. TOM AND PAT LEESON

VIII | ANIMAL TRADITIONS

BABY MAMMALS ARE BORN TO LEARN. They are the proverbial little sponges, eager to soak up information from their environment—the way mother smells, the feel of her teats and, more subtly, the way she behaves as a parent. Although few animals are as impressionable as young monkeys and apes, all mammals are affected by childhood events. For mice as for men, early experience provides the basis for lifelong habits and tastes.

For most mammalian infants, the principal source of information about the world is, quite naturally, their parent (or parents). When a deer fawn trails its mother through the woods, it benefits not only from her protection but also from her experience. Although animals are born with appropriate urges—an inclination to eat leaves and buds, say, rather

The nurturance that adult mammals offer to their young often includes a life-sustaining gift of experience. TOM AND PAT LEESON

OVERLEAF Summer offers a glistening array of greens, but not all are equally nourishing. This white-tailed fawn will learn what to select by observing and imitating its parent. ART WOLFE

than insects—their natural tendencies must be refined and shaped by specific knowledge. It is not enough to know that you like maple leaves, apples and cedar buds unless you also have an idea where and when these foods are to be found—high meadows in spring, valley bottoms in fall, brushy swamps in winter and so on. If a fawn had to draw this map by blundering around on its own, it would likely pay a high price for its ignorance. But by following closely on its mother's heels, a young deer positions itself to "feed" on her knowledge.

We're not talking about Bambi and his mom. "No, dear, don't eat that nasty dirt. Here, have a mouthful of these lovely lamb's quarters." The doe does not teach her youngster, but it learns anyway, as a natural result of mother-infant together- ness. This process, which is known to the experts as "social facilitation," is familiar to human parents as "having the kids underfoot." From a youngster's point of view, anything that inter- ests a grown-up might be worth checking out. Young rats, for example, don't even like to eat unless they are near adults or, at the very least, adult excrement (the ultimate in appetite enhance- ment). By following their parents' example, the pups learn not only what to eat but also, even more critically, what to avoid—like a food that some adult recently sniffed on the lips of a poisoned compatriot.

When novelty fails to present itself, the young create it for themselves, by getting up to all sorts of genial mischief.

To a greater or lesser extent, all young mammals pattern themselves on their care- givers. If the older generation acquires an unusual habit or skill, they may transmit it to their offspring as part of the local culture. Thus, rats in the Jerusalem pine forest of Israel feed on conifer seeds, which they strip out of the cones with a complex spiral technique. This behavior is so well established that you'd think it must be innate. Yet if a rat is raised in a lab, far from the pine woods, it will not have a clue about how to break into the cones. Instead, the skill must be learned during infancy in the interaction between parent and off- spring. By sticking its nose in its mother's way and grabbing cones from her mouth, a young rat quickly catches on to what is required. An inexperienced adult, by contrast, never picks up the skill, even if it is caged for months with an expert cone-stripper.

The weasel version of "in and out the window" seems to be a game for any number of players. ALAN AND SANDY CAREY

Generally speaking, young mammals are wide open to new experiences, much more so than adults. When novelty fails to present itself, the young create it for themselves by getting up to all sorts of genial mischief. Virtually every species of mammal has been known to play in its youth, from rats, bats and hedgehogs to zebras and bandicoots. Many animal sports are built around physical skills, like the startle-and-run games of elk calves—sudden outbursts of speed—that help prepare the youngsters to evade their enemies. Young right whales, on the other hand, practice moves they will need to mate by rolling over onto their backs as they later will for sex. Other games focus on serious social concerns, like the wild, romping play-fights that establish rank among wolves or the "King of the Castle" contests that many young mammals enjoy.

Virtually every species of mammal has been known to play in its youth, from rats, bats and hedgehogs to zebras and bandicoots.

But often play seems to be an end in itself, with no apparent purpose except to make something happen. Young monkeys, in particular, get up to crazy stunts, like tearing into a nest of stinging ants or "attacking" a treeful of hornbills and scaring them half to death. What will happen if I do that? What if I do it again? These random acts of silliness are not purposeless, because they throw up opportunities to develop physical skills, explore social relationships and flex the brain cells.

Every now and then, this playful, no-holds-barred approach to life turns up something entirely unexpected and useful. The most famous instance featured a bright-eyed little monkey—known to science as "Imo"—who made her first brilliant discovery at the age of eighteen months. Although Imo lived in the wilds of Koshima Islet, Japan, she and her troop were provided with extra food by a group of researchers. One day, as Imo was toying with a sweet potato, she took a sudden notion to wash it in a brook. Result: no more annoying sand in her mouth. Imo was so pleased with this improvement that she began washing sweet potatoes as a matter of course. Within months, the practice had spread to her favorite playmate, her mother and various other friends and relatives. A few years later, still as a juvenile, Imo invented a method for cleaning sand out of wheat. She would drop the grain into the water, wait for the grit to sink and then skim the floating wheat off the

This wizened infant in its woolly snowsuit is a baby Japanese macaque, or snow monkey. ART WOLFE

OVERLEAF Like big kitties playing with a mouse, these cheetah kittens harry a gazelle fawn under their mother's intent supervision. NORBERT ROSING

surface. This idea was also picked up by her kith and kin, who in turn passed it on to the next generation.

Again, there was no hint that Imo actively shared her innovations with her companions. She just did what she was doing, and they either caught on or not, depending on their interest and intelligence. Actual "teaching"—purposefully helping an individual learn something it needs to know—seems, at the very least, to be rare among animals. Apart from human children, young mammals have never been known to intentionally offer instruction to anyone. But what about adults?

Except for remarkable cases like the innovative Imo (who passed information "up" the generational chain to her elders), knowledge and skills usually flow "down" from experienced adults to naive juveniles. Until recently, ethologists have maintained that this transfer is always passive and unsophisticated. But some of the things that adult animals do are not easily explained by this minimalist theory. When an otter shoves her kits into the lake, does she want them to learn to swim? What else could possibly be her motivation? Similarly, when a cow moose slips away from her calf and hides till it finds her again, is she reinforcing and training its natural desire to follow her? Is she aware of this purpose?

Sadly, we cannot read animals' minds, but we can interpret their actions. Every now and then, we pick up hints that animal mothers know exactly what they are doing. Think, for example, of a female cheetah with a litter of baby kittens that must somehow be transformed into precise and deadly killers. Like other feline mothers (both wild and tame), the adult schools her youngsters by bringing home small animals for them to catch. Hares, which are very fleet of foot and likely to escape, are often maimed by the female before they are released. Gazelle fawns, however, are easier to retrieve and are usually presented to the youngsters with their faculties intact. When the kittens are small, the mother lets them harry the prey for only a few minutes before she makes the kill. But as her offspring become more proficient, she gives them the time they need to bring events to an appropriately bloody ending. In every case, her behavior is finely tuned to the circumstances, as if she has some awareness of what she is trying to accomplish.

Not surprisingly, the strongest evidence for teaching by nonhuman mammals comes

A mother bobcat takes a playful swat at her half-grown kitten. Is she consciously trying to sharpen its reflexes or simply enjoying a favorite feline sport? TOM AND PAT LEESON

from our closest relatives, the chimps. In the tropical rain forests of West Africa, chimpanzees use hammers and anvils to crack large, hard-shelled nuts. A good hammer stone is valued and subject to theft, so a wise owner keeps her tool kit where she can guard it. But if she is traveling with an infant of three or four years (the right age to take an interest in tools and their uses), she will start leaving her hammer on the anvil, where her youngster can find it. She may even set out a nut, as another token of her encouragement.

Although young chimps take up the challenge with enthusiasm, they are not immediately successful. (Nutcracking is a skilled trade that takes about ten years to perfect.) When a young apprentice runs into difficulties, its mother occasionally intervenes with expert tutelage. In one instance, a six-year-old juvenile broke into a panda nut and then put one of the hard-to-open inner kernels onto the anvil. Before he could strike it, his mother picked up the kernel, cleaned the anvil with her hand, and carefully repositioned the nut so that he could succeed in cracking it.

In another case, a five-year-old female spent the better part of ten minutes bashing at nuts with a poor-quality hammer stone. Her only reward was utter frustration. Alerted to the problem by her child's whimpering, her mother roused herself from a rest, ambled over and took the stone in her hand. Then, as the youngster watched, she slowly—ever so slowly—rotated the hammer into the most effective position, demonstrated its use and handed it back to her daughter. The age-old mammalian drama *Mother Knows Best* had just extended its run in the African rain forest.

The lesson for today: if you wave your tail in someone's face, you mustn't be too amazed if he or she takes the bait. DANIEL J. COX/NATURAL EXPOSURES

OVERLEAF Poised on the brink of success, an Alaska brown (or grizzly) bear demonstrates the art of still-fishing to an eager apprentice. TOM WALKER

IX | MAKING CONNECTIONS

THE TRANSFORMATION OF A HELPLESS NEWBORN into a competent adult is one of the commonplace miracles of human experience. Who would believe that the ambitious young woman with her own keys to "my" car was once a wide-eyed infant who cradled in my arms? Amazing in retrospect, this process can be excruciating to contemplate in advance. In the case nearest my heart, maturation has already been the work of 6,299 days (but who's counting?). A baby mouse, by contrast, may mature within one month. The smarter an animal is and the more it has to learn, the longer it will linger in the kingdom of childhood.

But whether growing up occupies a period of weeks or years, most young mammals

Even though it has been weaned, this young arctic fox (left) still looks to its mother for sustenance. By nudging her muzzle, the youngster puts in its request for a share of her stomach contents. NORBERT ROSING

eventually get the urge to wave good-bye to their parents and set out into the world. For animals as for humans, the passage from youth to adult life—from dependency to self-sufficiency—is fraught with difficulties. A beaver, for example, remains with its parents for almost two years and, during its second season, helps to care for its newborn siblings. The following spring (with a new batch of yearling assistants in the works), the parents decide that the two-year-old is surplus to their needs. Rebuffed and rejected by its family, the young adult embarks on an arduous journey, by both water and land, in search of a vacant pond and a breeding partner. If it succeeds in this risky quest, it will establish a colony of

For animals as for humans, the passage from youth to adult life—from dependency to self-sufficiency— is fraught with difficulties.

its own and take on the responsibilities of parenthood. If it fails, it will become a grim statistic, and that will be the end of that.

Among mammals in general, a high percentage of young adults die during their brief, transitional period of homelessness. This is true not only of beavers but also of skunks, bears, monkeys and a wide range of other animals. Starvation, predation and aggression by established adults all take their toll; so do human-imposed hazards such as traps and automobiles. As many as half of the young hopefuls that seek independence can be expected to perish in the attempt. Natural selection enforces a cruel decree that only the fit and the fortunate shall survive to breed.

For the most part, young adults face this ordeal alone, without assistance from the older generation. But in some species, parents are able to help their young through the difficult passage into adult life. Wolves, for example, give their youngsters the choice of remaining at home long after they are physically capable of reproduction. Although a few young adventurers disperse as soon as they're mature, others make a number of tentative, exploratory forays into the countryside before deciding what to do. Some of these animals ultimately choose to strike out on their own and take a chance on establishing their own packs. But others—perhaps young ne'er-do-wells that have little chance of success—turn their backs on this uncertain prospect. Forgoing the possibility of producing pups of their own, they stay with their parents and help care for their younger brothers and sisters. In return for this service and self-sacrifice, they are spared the hazards of life on the open

Elephant matriarchs may lead their herds for decades, providing leadership and care to their descendants and other group members.
DANIEL J. COX/NATURAL EXPOSURES

OVERLEAF Two massive bison cows pilot their calves through a misty spring morning in Yellowstone National Park. ALAN AND SANDY CAREY

road and are permitted to share the resources of the family home. If later—older and wiser—they decide to disperse, they may have a better chance of establishing themselves.

By allowing their grown-up offspring to join the family group, wolves extend parental care into adulthood. Something similar may also occur among wolves' preferred prey, the ungulates. Like wolves, many grazing animals—including tame and wild sheep, red deer (or elk), bison and African elephants—live in permanent, multigenerational social groupings. But whereas wolf packs include males and females, grazing animals practice a rigid segregation of the sexes. Young males typically wander off soon after they mature and travel alone or in loose, all-male aggregations. Daughters, on the other hand, generally remain in their natal groups, together with their mothers and sisters. Here, family ties can last for years, sometimes even for lifetimes.

By the age of two, a female sheep may be a mother and a grandmother, far beyond the stage at which we expect her to require the care of her own parent. Yet under some conditions, these animals continue to look to their mothers for guidance. The follow-the-leader behavior for which sheep are notorious is often the result of daughters that literally attempt to follow in their mothers' footsteps. (In a year-long study of one feral flock, fully half the instances of "following" met this description.) Although some mothers and daughters ignore each other completely, others stick together until parted by death. When the members of one tightly bonded duo were accidentally assigned to different flocks, the grown-up daughter squeezed herself under the intervening fence, intent on mother-daughter togetherness.

Nobody knows exactly how ewes benefit from keeping in touch with their mothers. It is no doubt telling, however, that the attachment seems to grow stronger when the animals are under threat from heavy predation or food shortage. In difficult times, the help and guidance of an older, more experienced animal may tip the balance in favor of survival and success. Among bison, we do know that mothers help their adult daughters to assert themselves in society. A young female on her own is oppressed by older cows that force her to accept slim pickings on the margins of the herd. But with her beefy mother clearly in

If this black bear cub is female, she may be allowed to forage on her mother's territory as an adult. By sharing what she has, a mother bear can help her daughters get established.

OVERLEAF This newborn harp seal will be weaned and abandoned by its mother at the tender age of two weeks. Will mother and infant meet again, in later life? Will they (like some other parent-offspring teams) show special regard for each other's wellbeing? JEFF FOOTT

evidence, she can muscle into the center of things and feed with the biggest and best.

Mothers that favor their adult daughters in these ways do so at a cost, because they are sharing resources they might otherwise claim exclusively for themselves. This altruism—a direct extension of maternal care—is the basis of most mammalian social systems. To paraphrase Edward O. Wilson, from his seminal text, *Sociobiology*, milk and mothering are the keys to understanding mammalian societies. When the relationship between mother and offspring persists beyond weaning, it provides a basis for the evolution of mutual caregiving.

Evolutionary biology tells us that the purpose of life is to ensure that our genes survive and prosper in future generations. But genes are not our personal property. They actually belong to our whole family line and exist in different individuals at the same time. (This, of course, is why baby Jimmy can be born with cousin Norbert's eyes.) The best way for a "selfish gene" to achieve its long-term goal may be to promote generosity among close relatives. This powerful principle, which is known as "kin selection" or "inclusive fitness," is as potent in practice as it is in theory. For example, female mice may nest communally, both in the wild and in the laboratory. The most fruitful partnerships—those that produce the most weaned pups—are nests that include mothers and daughters or two sisters. Even foster sisters (unrelated animals that have known each other since birth) are significantly less successful. A pair of strangers manages worst of all because they waste time and energy competing with each other.

Milk and mothering are the keys to understanding mammalian societies.

It is one thing to plop two mice in a cage and see how they get on. It is another to show that they would pair up with their relatives if they had to make the connection on their own. Do animals recognize their close kin? For the species that have been studied, the answer seems to be yes. Thus, when a female ground squirrel meets a total stranger, she will likely attack—unless the stranger happens to be a sister she has not seen since birth. In that case, the reunion will be peaceable or even cordial. This stranger carries a familiar scent, one that reminds her of her own body odor or perhaps, vaguely, of her

Although adult cheetahs are often described as "solitary," females spend their lives in the company of their offspring. Male kittens disperse at maturity, but daughters may stay on their mother's range (where they take care to keep out of each other's way).
DANIEL J. COX/NATURAL EXPOSURES

mother's amniotic fluid. A brother would likely be avoided on the same basis, since females prefer not to mate with close relatives.

Kinship recognition by mammals is poorly understood, but it probably originates in the intimate contact between mothers and their infants. Before and after birth, mothering is the matrix that holds littermates together where they can get to know both individual family members and general family characteristics. Deeply imprinted with this information, an animal may be able to identify not only members of its maternal lineage but also half siblings from its father's side. (Yet father and offspring may never have met.) This uncanny sensitivity to kinship is expressed in critical life decisions, such as the choice of mates, companions, enemies and allies.

The qualities we like best in ourselves, and that give us the greatest hope, have been bequeathed to us by our nature as parents.

Primates, as befits their rich social lives, have an especially acute and sophisticated awareness of family ties. According to primatologists Dorothy L. Cheney and Robert M. Seyfarth in their landmark book, *How Monkeys See the World*, vervet monkeys have a concept of relationship, through the maternal line, and understand that other individuals also have kinship bonds. Though subtle in principle, this understanding can be crude in its applications. In one typical instance, two little monkeys were fooling around, when one of them was wrestled to the ground. The loser's sister avenged this defeat by approaching the winner's sister (recognizable by her association with the same mother) and biting her on the tail.

From the petty to the profound, maternal connections are at the heart of primate social structures. In many species, a female's status in her troop—the single most important factor in determining her success—is directly inherited from her dam. From the moment of birth, the infant of a high-ranking female is treated with special respect and is sought after as a grooming partner and playmate. Within weeks, though still clearly a child, she can successfully challenge adults that are below her mother in rank. This has nothing to do with her own virtues or strengths; instead it derives solely from her mother's privilege. The youngster becomes a monkey aristocrat—a lifelong legacy of her parentage.

The parallels with humankind are all too obvious. The transmission of privilege (and poverty) between generations is one of our most intractable social problems. At least in part, it is a legacy of mammalian parental care which, for better or worse, permits us to extend our individual reach into the future. The sins or successes of parents are, indeed, liberally visited upon their progeny. As a species, we have been visited with the successes and failures of our mammalian ancestry. Chief among our inherited difficulties is the specialization of the female body—and not the male—for intensive parenting. What started out as a great advance in the swamps of the Mesozoic has become a hindrance to human progress in the twentieth century.

But if there are aspects of our inheritance we could live without, we have also been given the means to cope with our design flaws. Humans have been bequeathed a complex intelligence that is nurtured by our parents. We are smart because we are mammals, perhaps even clever enough to resolve the dilemmas that are posed by our mammalian inheritance. We have also been given a capacity for compassion and love, qualities that clearly relate to parental care. Because human infants invite the devotion of at least two caregivers, these "motherly" attributes have been inherited by both sexes. The qualities we like best in ourselves, and that give us our greatest hope, have been bequeathed to us by our nature as parents.

OVERLEAF **Taking full advantage of her extra-long limbs, this mother orangutan surrounds her infant with warmth.** ERWIN AND PEGGY BAUER

REFERENCES

General

The books and articles listed under this heading, as well as those marked with asterisks, were used repeatedly in the preparation of the text.

Clutton-Brock, T.H. *The Evolution of Parental Care.* Princeton, N.J.: Princeton University Press, 1991.

Elia, Irene. *The Female Animal.* Oxford: Oxford University Press, 1985.

Gubernick, David J., and Peter H. Klopfer. *Parental Care in Mammals.* New York: Plenum, 1981.

Gunderson, Harvey L. *Mammalogy.* New York: McGraw-Hill, 1976.

Krasnegor, Norman A., and Robert S. Bridges, eds. *Mammalian Parenting: Biochemical, Neurobiological, and Behavioral Determinants.* New York: Oxford University Press, 1990.

Macdonald, David, ed. *Encyclopedia of Mammals.* New York: Facts on File, 1984.

Moss, Cynthia. *Elephant Memories: Thirteen Years in the Life of an Elephant Family.* New York: William Morrow, 1988.

Reite, Martin, and Tiffany Field, eds. *The Psychobiology of Attachment and Separation.* Orlando: Academic Press, 1985.

Rheingold, Harriet L., ed. *Maternal Behavior in Mammals.* New York: John Wiley, 1963.

Savage, Arthur, and Candace Savage. *Wild Mammals of Western Canada.* Saskatoon: Western Producer Prairie Books, 1981.

Van Gelder, Richard G. *Biology of Mammals.* New York: Charles Scribner's Sons, 1969.

Vaughan, Terry A. *Mammalogy.* Philadelphia: Saunders College Publishing, 1986.

I Family Values

Carroll, Robert L. *Vertebrate Paleontology and Evolution.* New York: W.H. Freeman and Company, 1988.

Clutton-Brock, T.H., S.D. Albon, and F.E. Guinness. "Fitness Costs of Gestation and Lactation in Wild Mammals." *Nature* 337 (1989): 260–62.

Colbert, Edwin H. *Evolution of the Vertebrates: A History of the Backboned Animals through Time.* New York: Wiley-Liss, 1991.

*Hrdy, Sarah Blaffer. *The Woman That Never Evolved.* Cambridge: Harvard University Press, 1981.

Kemp, T.S. *Mammal-like Reptiles and the Origin of Mammals.* London: Academic Press, 1982.

Kermack, D.M., and K.A. Kermack. *The Evolution of Mammalian Characters.* London: Croom Helm, 1984.

Lillegraven, Jason A. "Reproduction in Mesozoic Mammals." In *Mesozoic Mammals: The First Two-Thirds of Mammalian History*, edited by Jason A. Lillegraven et al., 259–76. Berkeley: University of California Press, 1979.

———. "Why *Was* There a 'Marsupial-Placental Dichotomy?'" In *Mammals: Notes for a Short Course*, edited by P.D. Gingerich and C.E. Badgley, 72–86. University of Tennessee Department of Geological Sciences.

Neville, Margaret C., and Charles W. Daniel, eds. *The Mammary Gland: Development, Regulation, and Function.* New York: Plenum, 1987.

Pond, Caroline M. "The Significance of Lactation in the Evolution of Mammals." *Evolution* 31 (1977): 177–99.

Ramsey, Elizabeth M. *The Placenta: Human and Animal.* New York: Praeger, 1982.

Wynn, Ralph M., and William P. Jollie, eds. *Biology of the Uterus.* New York: Plenum, 1989.

II Ab Ovo

Clark, Mertice M., Peter Karpluk, and Bennett G. Galef Jr. "Hormonally Mediated Inheritance of Acquired Characteristics in Mongolian Gerbils." *Nature* 364 (1993): 712.

Clutton-Brock, T.H., and G.R. Iason. "Sex Ratio Variation in Mammals." *Quarterly Review of Biology* 61 (1986): 339–74.

Gosling, L.M. "Selective Abortion of Entire Litters in the Coypu: Adaptive Control of Offspring Production in Relation to Quality and Sex." *American Naturalist* 127 (1986): 772–95.

Hoefs, Manfred, and Uli Nowlan. "Distorted Sex Ratios in Young Ungulates: The Role of Nutrition." *Journal of Mammalogy* 75 (1994): 631–36.

Huck, U. William, Jon Seger, and Robert D. Lisk. "Litter Sex Ratios in the Golden Hamster Vary with Time of Mating and Litter Size and Are Not Binomially Distributed." *Behavioral Ecology and Sociobiology* 26 (1990): 99–109.

"In the Womb." *Discover* 12 (May 1991): 14–16.

Meikle, D.B., J.H. Kruper, and C.R. Browning. "Adult Male House Mice Born to Undernourished Mothers Are Unattractive to Oestrous Females." *Animal Behaviour* 50 (1995): 753–58.

Mendl, Michael, Adroaldo J. Zanella, Donald M. Broom, and Colin T. Whittemore. "Maternal Social Status and Birth Sex Ratio in Domestic Pigs: An Analysis of Mechanisms." *Animal Behaviour* 50 (1995): 1361–70.

Moses, Richard W., Graham J. Hickling, and John S. Millar. "Variation in Sex Ratios of

Offspring in Wild Bushy-Tailed Woodrats."
Journal of Mammalogy 76 (1995): 1047–55.

Samson, Claude, and Jean Huot. "Reproductive
Biology of Female Black Bears in Relation to
Body Mass in Early Winter." *Journal of
Mammalogy* 76 (1995): 68–77.

Trivers, Robert L., and Dan E. Willard. "Natural
Selection of Parental Ability to Vary the Sex
Ratio of Offspring." *Science* 179 (1973): 90–91.

Vandenbergh, John G. "And Brother Begat
Nephew." *Nature* 364 (1993): 671–72.

Wiley, David N., and Phillip J. Clapham. "Does
Maternal Condition Affect the Sex Ratio of
Offspring in Humpback Whales?" *Animal
Behaviour* 46 (1993): 321–24.

III That's My Baby

Cochrum, Lendell. *Introduction to Mammalogy.*
New York: Ronald Press, 1962.

*Ewer, R. F. *Ethology of Mammals.* London: Logos,
1968.

Eyer, Diane E. *Mother-Infant Bonding: A Scientific
Fiction.* New Haven: Yale University Press,
1992.

Gustin, Mary K., and Gary F. McCracken.
"Scent Recognition Between Females and
Pups in the Bat *Tadarida brasiliensis mexicana.*"
Animal Behaviour 35 (1987): 13–19.

Habib, Marlene. "Parent-Child Bonding Key to
Development." *Saskatoon Star-Phoenix*, May
11, 1966, p. C18.

Mowat, Garth, Brian G. Slough, and Stan
Boutin. "Lynx Recruitment During a
Snowshoe Hare Population Peak and
Decline in Southwest Yukon." *Journal of
Wildlife Management* 60 (1996): 441–52.

Romeyer, Alain, et al. "Maternal Labelling Is
Not Necessary for the Establishment of
Discrimination between Kids by Recently
Parturient Goats." *Animal Behaviour* 46 (1993):

705–12.

"A Rush of Maternal Feelings to the Brain." *New
Scientist* 120 (December 3, 1988): 34.

Vines, Gail. "Ewe-Turn for Maternal Behaviour."
New Scientist 134 (May 16,1992): 14.

IV Motherhood Issues

Alleva, Enrico, Antonio Caprioli, and Giovanni
Laviola. "Litter Gender Composition Affects
Maternal Behavior of the Primiparous Mouse
Dam (*Mus musculus*)." *Journal of Comparative
Psychology* 103 (1989): 83–87.

*Berman, Carol M. "Intergenerational
Transmission of Maternal Rejection Rates
Among Free-Ranging Rhesus Monkeys."
Animal Behaviour 39 (1990): 329–37.

Coppinger, Raymond P., and Charles Kay
Smith. "A Model for Understanding the
Evolution of Mammalian Behavior."
Current Mammalogy 1 (1987): 335–74.

*Dolhinow, Phyllis. "Tactics of Primate
Immaturity." In *Man and Beast Revisited*, edited
by Michael H. Robinson and Lionel Tiger,
139–57. Washington: Smithsonian
Institution Press, 1991.

Hofer, Myron A. "Parental Contributions to
the Development of Their Offspring." In
Parental Care in Mammals, edited by David J.
Gubernick and Peter H. Klopfer, 77–115,
New York: Plenum, 1981.

Hrdy, Sarah Blaffer. "Sex-Biased Parental
Investment Among Primates and Other
Mammals: A Critical Evaluation of the
Trivers-Willard Hypothesis." In *Child Abuse
and Neglect: Biosocial Dimensions*, edited by
Richard J. Gelles and Jane B. Lancaster,
97–147. New York: Aldine de Gruyter, 1987.

*Jolly, Alison. *The Evolution of Primate Behavior.* New
York: Macmillan, 1972.

Lorenz, Konrad. "Part and Parcel in Animal and

Human Societies (1950): A Methodological
Discussion." In *Studies in Animal and Human
Behaviour*, vol. 2, translated by Robert
Martin, 153–62. London: Methuen, 1972.

*Masson, Jeffrey, and Susan McCarthy. *When
Elephants Weep: The Emotional Lives of Animals.*
London: Jonathan Cape, 1994.

"New Home Cat's Meow for Heroic Feline,"
Saskatoon Star-Phoenix, June 29, 1996, p. A18.

Schwede, Georg, Hubert Hendrichs, and
Christen Wemmer. "Early Mother-Young
Relations in White-Tailed Deer." *Journal of
Mammalogy* 75 (1994): 438–45.

Short, Roger. "Elephants and Birth Control."
New Scientist 135 (August 1992): 21–23.

*Suomi, Stephen J. "Adolescent Depression
and Depressive Symptoms: Insights from
Longitudinal Studies with Rhesus Monkeys."
Journal of Youth and Adolescence 20 (1991):
273–87.

V Liquid Assets

Barrett, Louise, and Robin Dunbar. "Not Now,
Dear, I'm Busy." *New Scientist* 142 (1994):
30–33.

Gomendio, Montserrat. "Parent/Offspring
Conflict and Maternal Investment in Rhesus
Macaques." *Animal Behaviour* 42 (1991):
993–1005.

Hass, Christine C. "Alternative Maternal-care
Patterns in Two Herds of Bighorn Sheep."
Journal of Mammalogy 7 (1990): 24–35.

Hauser, Marc D., and Lynn A. Fairbanks.
"Mother-Offspring Conflict in Vervet
Monkeys: Variation in Response to
Ecological Conditions." *Animal Behaviour* 36
(1988): 802–13.

Hofer, Herbert, and Marion L. East. "The
Commuting System of Serengeti Spotted
Hyaenas: How a Predator Copes with

Migratory Prey." *Animal Behaviour* 46 (1993): 575–89.

Hoogland, J.L., R.H. Tamarin, and C.K. Levy. "Communal Nursing in Prairie Dogs." *Behavioral Ecology and Sociobiology* 24 (1989): 91–95.

*Hrdy, Sarah Blaffer. "Natural-born Mothers." *Natural History* no. 12 (1995): 30–42.

Jacquot, Joseph J., and Stephen H. Vessey. "Non-Offspring Nursing in the White-Footed Mouse, *Peromyscus leucopus*." *Animal Behaviour* 48 (1994): 1236–40.

Laurenson, M. Karen. "Behavioural Costs and Constraints of Lactation in Free-Living Cheetahs." *Animal Behaviour* 50 (1995): 815–26.

Lydersen, Christian, and Kit M. Kovacs. "Diving Behaviour of Lactating Harp Seal, *Phoca groenlandica*, Females from the Gulf of St. Lawrence, Canada." *Animal Behaviour* 46 (1993): 1213–21.

Oftedal, Olav T., Daryl J. Boness, and Raymond A. Tedman. "The Behavior, Physiology, and Anatomy of Lactation in the Pinnipedia." In *Current Mammalogy*, edited by Hugh H. Genoways, vol. 1, 175–243. New York: Plenum, 1987.

Packer, Craig, Susan Lewis, and Anne Pusey. "A Comparative Analysis of Non-Offspring Nursing." *Animal Behaviour* 43 (1992): 265–81.

*Rachlow, Janet L., and R. Terry Bowyer. "Variability in Maternal Behavior by Dall's Sheep: Environmental Tracking or Adaptive Strategy?" *Journal of Mammalogy* 75 (1994): 328–37.

Worlein, Julie M., G. Gray Eaton, Deanne F. Johnson, and Barbara B. Glick. "Mating Season Effects on Mother-Infant Conflict in Japanese Macaques, *Macaca fuscata*." *Animal Behaviour* 36 (1988): 1472–81.

VI What about Dad?

Burne, Jerome. "Love in a Cold Climate Dents Monkeys' Macho Image." *New Scientist* 145 (February 1995): 15.

Daly, Martin. "Why Don't Male Mammals Lactate?" *Journal of Theoretical Biology* 78 (1979): 325–45.

Francis, Charles M., Edythe L.P. Anthony, Jennifer A. Brunton, and Thomas H. Kunz. "Lactation in Male Fruit Bats." *Nature* 367 (1994): 691–92.

Gubernick, David J. "A Maternal Chemosignal Maintains Paternal Behaviour in the Biparental California Mouse, *Permosycus californicus*." *Animal Behaviour* 39 (1990): 936–42.

Gubernick, David J., and Jeffrey R. Alberts. "Postpartum Maintenance of Paternal Behaviour in the Biparental California Mouse, *Peromyscus californicus*." *Animal Behaviour* 37 (1989): 656–64.

Gubernick, David J., Sandra L. Wright, and Richard E. Brown. "The Significance of Father's Presence for Offspring Survival in the Monogamous California Mouse, *Peromyscus californicus*." *Animal Behaviour* 46 (1993): 539–46.

Hector, Anne C. Keddy, Robert M. Seyfarth, and Michael J. Raleigh. "Male Parental Care, Female Choice and the Effect of an Audience in Vervet Monkeys." *Animal Behaviour* 38 (1989): 262–71.

Lyons, Jill P. "Effects of Biparental Care and Age of Stimulus Pups on Care-giving by Male and Female Virgin Mice, *Mus musculus*." *Animal Behaviour* 48 (1994): 228–31.

McGrew, W.C. "Parental Division of Infant Caretaking Varies with Family Composition in Cotton-Top Tamarins." *Animal Behaviour* 36 (1988): 285–86.

"Mr. Mom." *Discover* (May 1991): 18.

Oliveras, Diana, and Melinda Novak.

"A Comparison of Paternal Behaviour in the Meadow Vole *Microtus pennsylvanicus*, the Pine Vole *M. Pinetorum* and the Prairie Vole *M. Ochrogaster*." *Animal Behaviour* 34 (1986): 519–26.

*Paul, Andreas, Jutta Kuester, and Joachim Arnemann. "The Sociobiology of Male-Infant Interactions in Barbary Macaques, *Macaca sylvanus*." *Animal Behaviour* 51 (1996): 155–70.

Perrigo, Glenn, W. Cully Bryant, and Frederick S. vom Saal. "A Unique Neural Timing System Prevents Male Mice from Harming Their Own Offspring." *Animal Behaviour* 39 (1990): 535–39.

Price, Eluned C. "Infant Carrying as a Courtship Strategy of Breeding Male Cotton-Top Tamarins." *Animal Behaviour* 40 (1990): 785–86.

———. "Sex and Helping: Reproductive Strategies of Breeding Male and Female Cotton-Top Tamarins, *Saguins oedipus*." *Animal Behaviour* 43 (1992): 717–28.

Pryce, C.R. "Individual and Group Effects on Early Caregiver-Infant Relationships in Red-Bellied Tamarin Monkeys." *Animal Behaviour* 36 (1988): 1455–64.

Schug, Malcolm D., Stephen H. Vessey, and Eileen M. Underwood. "Paternal Behavior in a Natural Population of White-Footed Mice (Peromyscus leucopus)." *American Midland Naturalist* 127 (1992): 373–80.

Storey, Anne E., Carole G. Bradbury, and Tammy L. Joyce. "Nest Attendance in Male Meadow Voles: The Role of the Female in Regulating Male Interactions with Pups." *Animal Behaviour* 47 (1994): 1037–46.

Storey, Anne E., and Tammy L. Joyce. "Pup Contact Promotes Paternal Responsiveness in Male Meadow Voles." *Animal Behaviour* 49 (1995): 1–10.

Taub, David Milton, ed. *Primate Paternalism.* New

York: Van Nostrand Reinhold, 1984.

Wang, Zuoxin, and Melinda A. Novak. "Alloparental Care and the Influence of Father Presence on Juvenile Prairie Voles, *Microtus ochrogaster*." *Animal Behaviour* 47 (1994): 281–88.

Wynne-Edwards, Katherine E. "Biparental Care in Djungarian but Not Siberian Dwarf Hamsters (*Phodopus*)." *Animal Behaviour* 95 (1995): 1571–85.

VII Honey, I Ate the Kids

*Hausfater, Glenn, and Sarah Blaffer Hrdy, eds. *Infanticide: Comparative and Evolutionary Persectives*. New York: Aldine, 1984.

McLeod, Peter J. "Infanticide by Female Wolves." *Canadian Journal of Zoology* 68 (1990): 402–404.

*Parmigianni, Stefano, and Frederick S. vom Saal, eds. *Infanticide and Parental Care*. Chur, Switzerland: Harwood Academic, 1994.

Pierotti, Raymond. "Infanticide Versus Adoption: An Intergenerational Conflict." *American Naturalist* 138 (1991): 1140–58.

Reidman, Marianne L. "The Evolution of Alloparental Care and Adoption in Mammals and Birds." *Quarterly Review of Biology* 57 (1982): 405–31.

Salo, Allen L., and Jeffrey A. French. "Early Experience, Reproductive Success, and Development of Parental Behaviour in Mongolian Gerbils." *Animal Behaviour* 38 (1989): 693–702.

VIII Animal Traditions

Barnett, S.A. "The 'Instinct to Teach.'" *Nature* 220 (1968): 747–49.

Boesch, Christophe. "Teaching among Wild Chimpanzees." *Animal Behaviour* 41 (1991): 530–32.

Capitanio, John P. "Early Experience and Social Processes in Rhesus Macaques (*Macaca mulatta*): I. Dyadic Social Interaction." *Journal of Comparative Psychology* 98 (1984): 35–44.

Caro, T.M., and M.D. Hauser. "Is There Teaching in Nonhuman Animals?" *Quarterly Review of Biology* 67 (1992): 151–74.

Fagen, Robert. *Animal Play Behavior*. New York: Oxford University Press, 1981.

*Hrdy, Sarah Blaffer. *The Woman That Never Evolved*. Cambridge: Harvard University Press, 1981.

Maestripieri, Dario. "Maternal Encouragement of Infant Locomotion in Pigtail Macaques, *Macaca nemestrina*." *Animal Behaviour* 51 (1996): 603–10.

———. "Maternal Encouragement in Nonhuman Primates and the Question of Animal Teaching." *Human Nature* 6 (1995): 361–78.

Mainardi, Danilo, and Marisa Mainardi. "Culture and Genetics in the House Mouse." In *Social Learning: Psychological and Biological Perspectives*, edited by Thomas R. Zentall and Bennett G. Galef Jr., 239–52. Hillsdale, N.J.: Lawrence Erlbaum, 1988.

Nishida, Toshisada. "Local Traditions and Cultural Transmission." In *Primate Societies*, edited by Barbara B. Smuts, et al., 462–74. Chicago: University of Chicago Press, 1987.

Vines, Gail. "Some Baboons Like It Wet." *New Scientist* 135 (1992): 15.

IX Making Connections

*Cheney, Dorothy L., and Robert M. Seyfarth. *How Monkeys See the World: Inside the Mind of Another Species*. Chicago: University of Chicago Press, 1990.

Green, Wendy C.H., Joseph G. Griswold, and Aron Rothstein. "Post-weaning Associations among Bison Mothers and Daughters." *Animal Behaviour* 38 (1989): 847–58.

Hepper, Peter G. "The Amniotic Fluid: An Important Priming Role in Kin Recognition." *Animal Behaviour* 35 (1987): 1343–46.

———, ed. *Kin Recognition*. Cambridge: Cambridge University Press, 1991.

L'Heureux, Nathalie, Mauro Lucherini, Marco Festa-Bianchet, and Jon T. Jorgenson. "Density-Dependent Mother-Yearling Association in Bighorn Sheep." *Animal Behaviour* 49 (1995): 901–10.

Holmes, Warren G. "Kin Recognition by Phenotype Matching in Female Belding's Ground Squirrels." *Animal Behaviour* 34 (1986): 38–47.

Porter, Richard H., John A. Matochik, and Jennifer W. Makin. "Discrimination between Full-Sibling Spiny Mice (*Acomys cahirinus*) by Olfactory Signatures." *Animal Behaviour* 34 (1986): 1182–88.

Rowell, T.E. "Till Death Us Do Part: Long-Lasting Bonds between Ewes and Their Daughters." *Animal Behaviour* 42 (1991): 681–82.

*Wilson, Edward O. *Sociobiology: The New Synthesis*. Cambridge: Belknap/Harvard University Press, 1975.

Wu, Hannah M.H., Warren G. Holmes, Steven R. Medina, and Gene P. Sackett. "Kin Preference in Infant *Macaca nemestrina*." *Nature* 285 (1980): 225–27.

INDEX